AF521593

AUSTRALIAN PUBS

AUSTRALIAN PUBS

text
JOHN LARKINS
photographs
BRUCE HOWARD

RIGBY

RIGBY LIMITED • ADELAIDE • SYDNEY
MELBOURNE • BRISBANE • PERTH
First published 1973
Reprinted April 1974

Library of Congress Catalog Card Number 79–183431
National Library of Australia Card Number and ISBN 0 85179 620 6

Wholly designed and set up in Australia
Printed in Singapore by McGraw-Hill Far Eastern Publishers (S) Ltd.

Contents

Australian pubs

This has been thirsty work. Many thousands of glasses have been emptied since the day we announced to our wives: "We're going on a 25,000-mile pub crawl. Don't wait up!" Our expedition began in the public bar of the Silverton Hotel, near Broken Hill, one hot Sunday evening and ended nearly a year later in the Wrest Point Casino, under snow-capped Mount Wellington. In that time we washed more outback dust down our throats than most city dwellers would in a lifetime. We made hundreds of friends, and we hope those who read this book will have the opportunity to meet those same people some day.

Perhaps there are a few who might doubt the veracity of some of these tales. But we, in our innocence, prefer to believe they are all absolutely true!

We would like to acknowledge the help of several companies that believed it was not impossible for two men to embark on the greatest pub crawl in history and survive: Australian Hotels' Association, Courage Breweries Ltd, General Motors-Holden's Pty Ltd, Alcoa of Australia Ltd, and the Swan Brewery Co. And also of all the publicans, barmaids, and plain old blokes at the bar.

The Hero of Waterloo

In the pub's bowels, deep below the gay crowd's dancing feet, an awful six-by-four cell is carved into the solid rock. The rusted chains which held its outcast occupants to the cold walls 170 years ago still remain. On this cold October evening in the 1970s the cell contains nothing more mournful than empty beer kegs (though there are some sincere drinkers who would say there can be nothing more mournful than an empty keg). With the help of a torch-light, the hardy visitor to this dungeon, this menacing hole sliced from the rock face, can see the outline of a trapdoor in the ceiling. And thereby hangs a tale of man's inhumanity to man.

On the wall of the bar upstairs, some mid-twentieth century youth, perhaps feeling as alone and unwanted as the souls who once languished in chains beneath, has scribbled: "Oh, damn! I am not a rag or bone to be thrown away for nothing."

This is the ancient Hero of Waterloo, perched in the Sydney district known as the Rocks. Now, there are arguments about the Hero. Is it the oldest pub in the city? But wasn't it delicensed for years? It wasn't always a pub, though, was it? Oh, who cares. What do exact dates matter? What does matter is that the Hero isn't much younger than Sydney itself, and it remains surely one of the ten best pubs in the land.

THE HERO OF WATERLOO HOTEL.
THE HERO OF
WATERLOO
TOOTHS
RESCHS
TOOTHS
RESCHS

Come to the Hero late one weekday morning, sit yourself down on a stool in the corner, and observe the unlikely blend of people the old place draws. First come the grimy wharfies up from the docks, then others are fluttering among them, fashionable girls from the skyscraper offices and their smart young escorts. The wharfies drift away, the odd young executive, a late luncher, remains behind in muted conversation with his companions. And the pub falls asleep for an hour or so. Then they come again, the in-crowd, shoving, jostling, laughing, calling for the house red, and wisecracking with the publican, Bill Smith.

Darkness comes, and the band is thumping away—a tea chest bass, a man thumping two lumps of wood together, and not much else. And the loners are already spreading their messages across the wall at the very end of the bar—"leave no turn unstoned," "blow your nose, not your brain," "Dave is depressed," "the end of the world has been postponed for forty days owing to the lack of trumpet players," "one thing I know for sure is that I know nothing . . ." And the masterpiece graffiti: "Attention! This wall will soon be available in paper-back!" Such a publishing event would surprise no one in the bar. They are a modern crowd. But they are drawn to the most venerable pub.

Take that indolent young man there—does he know where he is standing? Does he know the story of that trapdoor? Bill Smith does: "In the early 1800s, the idea was to get a bloke full of booze and stand 'im over that trapdoor. Then they'd slip him a Mickey Finn, see, open the trapdoor and drop 'im into the cellar. They'd cart 'im along a tunnel cut through the limestone right to the harbour, and when he'd wake up with a raging hangover, he'd be at sea. That's how they shanghaied blokes to serve on ships. One thing, though, I can't find that tunnel—it's cut in the rocks somewhere."

And what about that granite bath in the cellar? "The story goes," Bill said, "that the secretary to Governor Macquarie was such a bastard that he knew some of the soldiers wanted to kill him. So he made the cellar his quarters and bathed in that granite tub. We still get a bit of use out of it today. Crowds of youngsters like to hire the cellar for parties and bucks turns. They fill up the bath with champagne and drink it with straws. The young blokes like to manacle the groom in the convict cell and leave 'im there. Just a prank really. Oh, I know about the historical importance of this cellar, but I don't think the youngsters can do any harm. All the spew and whatnot, it all washes out."

The Hero is thought to have been originally built, presumably with convict labour, as a barracks in 1804. By 1815 it was licensed in the name of The Little Princess, and the name was changed to its present one after the victory at Waterloo.

Muriel

The wind howled its lament across the drought country, through the gasping trees beside the track, and raised a flurry of dust from a road cracked like the lips of a man lost in a blazing desert. On the pub verandah, the red dust coated the mattresses on the metal beds. Was the place deserted? God, you could do with a beer, and there was nothing for fifty miles each side of this place. On the map it simply said "Hamilton Hotel." Oh, sure, someone had warned way back in Winton: "You'd better be careful. I heard the people who have that place were trying to get out. You wanna make sure they're still there." Surely they hadn't gone?

Muriel Britton finally answered the cries. "Anyone here, anyone here?" She'd been lying down and she came to the bar pushing back her hair and straightening her dress. She had that tired, dry, wan look of outback women in hard times.

"I haven't sold a beer for days," she said, "I'm just waiting to go. The good days have gone. I'm alone here now. The drought's just about wiped everyone out. We used to have hundreds of shearers come through here. I remember old blokes who came in with £300 pay in their pockets and they'd set about drinking it all. After a few weeks, they'd say: 'How long have I been here?' 'About six weeks.' 'C'mon, it can't be that long—maybe a couple of days.' 'No, six weeks.'

"Gosh, they were in a bad way. Some wouldn't even leave their beds. They'd just sing out for me to bring a beer. After a couple of weeks, I'd have to shave them—they shook so much they had to use handkerchiefs to hold their beers steady."

She looked at the sky. "It might rain. You going to Boulia? Well, you'd better start moving before it comes down. Just a couple of points, and you'll be stuck on that track for days." There was no stock on the road west—just five thin emus. And it didn't rain after all.

HOTEL HAMILTON

Warren in the pink

There's a bar in the National Hotel, Brisbane, where the idle drinker can cast a lewd glance at the mirrors on the ceiling and be rewarded with a splendid view right down the barmaid's ample cleavage. A truly brilliant idea, but it is not the main attraction at the National.

The great attraction is Warren. Warren dispenses drinks and advice from a cloud of pink lighting. His fingernails are painted black, his dress is superb, his eyebrows are plucked, and his makeup is immaculate. Warren is charming. He never, but never, loses his cool. He is, perhaps, Brisbane's busiest amateur psychologist, everyone's gentle confidant. His own little bar is on the ground floor, just off the street. Creep in, lonely people, and unburden yourself to Warren. He understands, he'll listen.

Warren knows everything. "Oh, Warren, what should I do about it, then?"

"Perhaps a little less mascara, dear."

She is fortyish but she unleashes a schoolgirl's smile of gratitude. "Do you think so, oh, do you?" Everyone believes Warren.

For thirteen years he reigned supreme at the Rainbow cocktail bar at Lennon's. The National seduced him away, gave him his own splendid pink bar, Warren's Bar, and insured him for a rumoured $50,000. It is said that he is the highest-paid barman in Queensland, probably in the whole of Australia, but Warren would consider such talk positively vulgar.

His clientele are an unlikely mixture. He freely admits to having stolen them away from Lennons when he shifted.

NATIONAL HOTEL

"I don't know what my success secret is," he said, "if I have one at all. I'm a talker, a friend. When the wool buyers come from Sydney and Melbourne, they always visit me. I have so many friends from the station properties." And here, you can sense that Warren just might be a snob—in the nicest sort of way, of course.

"The lonely people come to talk to me. A man came, he was a visitor from another city, and after a few days he said, 'Gee, this is a dead town,' and I said, 'Oh, cut it out, Lance, just give me two days.' So I introduced him to people. I'm always doing that. He said later, 'I've had the best time of my life.' "

There's a story around that Warren's a great fighter. "Never tangle with him," they mutter. But Warren throws up his hands in horror. "Oh, no! Not at all. But I was quite sporting as a boy. I played rugby and Australian rules."

But the rumour of his punching prowess persists, and for that reason Warren does not have to tolerate as many sly remarks as one might expect to be delivered to a barman who wears makeup and painted fingernails. "You do hear some dirty things, of course, but you ignore them." He presses his fingertips together and purses his lips. The subject is closed.

Warren mixes his Southerly Buster for a male customer and a special concoction for his female companion—bitters, lime, gin, and a dash of white Curacao.

He passes it across: "That's called a 'Young Lady,' " he smiles, "for a young lady."

She is overcome. What style the man has.

Every evening, an hour and a half before his own bar opens, Warren takes up position on a stool in one of the National's seventeen other bars. "That is my social time. I receive people. They come to weep on my shoulder. I rarely go to a party after work so people who wish to see me know they can find me before I start work.

"There are, as you might imagine, newcomers who come and stare at me and say, 'Is it real?' and such things, but after we've had a drink and a talk they understand that, well, put it this way, although I dress up camp, I don't act camp. My old friends come and say, 'Oh, Warren, I haven't seen you for ten years, and you haven't a line in your face. How *do* you do it?' "

Is the camp bit a gimmick?

"Well, in a way it is. But the reason I started wearing makeup, you know, is that I've got a very heavy beard. Half an hour after I've had a shave, I need another one. Anyway, one day some chaps from J. C. Williamson's said, 'Why don't you try stage makeup?' so I did and I've been wearing it ever since 1948.

Oh, I go to the shops with it on. I'm forty-six, but say I look younger, go on. A lot of people don't believe that I was in the army in New Guinea in 1943. I typed at 110 words a minute, and they needed clerks so I got a sort of secretarial job. I had my own desk and two native boys to clean my boots and look after my two jeeps. It was marvellous. Do you realise that I've been wearing makeup a lot longer than many of the women who come in? I'm always happy to give them advice, but only if they ask for it, of course. Eyebrow shaving, things like that.

"If I know them personally, I'll go to their place after work and do their eyebrows and teach them how to apply makeup. My life is this hotel and the people who come here. It is my complete existence. I have my own house, a war-service home in Camp Hill, but I only go there to watch television, cook my little meals, and do my washing. You asked me how much I thought I meant to this hotel. I can only tell you that I can mean no more to it than it means to me."

Warren Bardsley Dennis, named after the Test cricketer, is a thoroughly nice person who'll welcome you at any time.

Oh, and if you're shouting, he'll have a small beer with sarsaparilla.

The Stockyard Bar, Lennon's Hotel

Surveyor-General Inn

She was pretty, so they say, in a wanton sort of way, and not yet thirty, but they hanged her behind the sandstone walls of Berrima jail on 22 October 1842—and now the ghost of Lucretia Dunkley haunts the pub across the paddock. Old Weir (he's the one in the corner with the port) knows she's there, somewhere, and the publican, Etta D'Arrietta, whispers: "I would not sleep in the inn unless someone else were staying here, too." When the time comes for a man to drain his last glass and make his solitary way into the darkness, many a red eye has gazed nervously at the fireplace in the public bar where Lucretia is most likely to appear—in filmy white with the head of the lover who died with her under her arm. But let us return to Lucretia later.

The Surveyor-General Inn at Berrima, eighty-seven miles south-west of Sydney, was built in 1835, the same year the jail was started, and is the oldest continually-licensed inn in Australia. In the cellar are rings which held the chains of the miserable convicts who built the pub and the jail, and some of the bricks inside the pub bear their thumb prints.

It seems that Lucretia, her husband Henry, and a dashing, young ticket-of-leave man, Martin Beech, were living on a farm at Gunning, not far away. The handsome Beech soon seduced Lucretia (without having to ask twice, according to local gossip) and soon he was cheerfully cuckolding the hapless Henry. But Beech wanted more. Did he want Henry's farm as well as his wife? Anyway, he murdered Henry. The outraged populace quickly saw to it that the temptress was dragged to the gallows with her lover. Why is it that the descendants of those good citizens who put the noose around Lucretia's neck are so concerned with

her today? Do they worry, perhaps, that she was not so strongly implicated after all? And why did one young man's hair turn white overnight when he saw her sitting on his car?

Mrs D'Arrietta said: "I didn't believe in ghosts when I came here, but about three years ago there was the sound of someone crying. And there was the time we were having a party and we heard the electric organ in the bar. I looked around and no one was missing from the party. Another night we heard strange sounds, and I crept from my bed and followed the dog upstairs. He paused on a landing, bristled, and wouldn't go any further. We saw nothing, but he did.

Some ghost-hunters came and took a picture of her in the fireplace. I saw it."

Lucretia, according to the most reliable information, frequents a bedroom on the first floor where Mrs D'Arrietta, anxious to maintain good relations with her, has installed a giant brass bed. Two valiant ladies came from Canberra, reserved the big brass bed, and went to the bar to imbibe sufficient courage to confront Lucretia. The locals would brook no interference with their ghost and induced the ladies into a charming state of intoxication, whereupon they spent the night on the big brass bed, snoring lustily while Lucretia, no doubt, skipped freely past their sodden bodies with Mr Beech's head clasped firmly under her arm.

Anyone with enough nerve can sleep in that room, and a very scandalous room it is, too. A nineteenth-century Governor of New South Wales was known to have spent a night of heavy breathing there with a winsome young chambermaid, and she became heavy with child (or in the puddin' club, whichever way you like it) within the statutory time. Her father was a pugilist of some note and he set off for Sydney to seek an interview with the governor, but not, to everyone's surprise, to leave His Excellency with a lip as swollen as young what's-her-name's tummy. He demanded and received sufficient cash to hush the matter up, and the scandal never really developed the way it should have, damn it.

Mrs D'Arrietta is doing marvellous work restoring the inn—and trying to make Lucretia as comfortable as possible. Is Lucretia pleased? At night there are sometimes strange winds. Perhaps it is Lucretia whistling her approval. They only hope she's not hissing.

Craig's

Craig's was a child of the Golden Age, the wonderful, bawdy 1850s when men drew gold from the earth by the ton and Ballarat had nearly as many people as Sydney. Thomas Bath brought wood and iron from Geelong, bluestone ballast from England, and rock quarried from the extinct volcanic crater on Mount Buninyong, a few miles away. And in June 1853 Bath's Ballarat Hotel was built. So successful was his venture that he was adding another two stories by December.

There were no mineshafts under the hotel so he had a massive bluestone cellar which, today, has been turned into a bar by the present owners, Dudley Erwin, M.P., former Federal Minister for Air, and his wife, and Mr Steve Jacobi. Bath gave the town something else of which to be proud, a tower atop the pub with a clock that could be seen by miners on their claims for some distance around. In 1856 the hotel served as a temporary town hall and later, as a mark of gratitude, Bath was given a private road between the hotel and the permanent town hall

building. Bath's Lane still exists today. At the corner of Lydiard and Sturt streets, not far from the hotel, was the Cobb & Co. office, and this corner was known simply as "Cobb's Corner."

Walter Craig, a noted sportsman and lover of fine horseflesh, took over the hotel in 1857. He called the pub Craig's and later, Craig's Royal Hotel, probably to mark the visit of Prince Alfred in 1867.

Craig entered a horse, Nimblefoot, in the 1870 Melbourne Cup and wagered three cigars to $1,000 with a bookmaker, Jeremiah Slack, that the horse would win.

However, several days before the race, Craig dreamed the horse would win the race, but the jockey would be wearing a black armband. He related this dream to friends.

On the morning of the race, Walter Craig dropped dead. Nimblefoot won—and the jockey wore a black armband in mourning. Slack paid the bet to his family.

Craig's passed through a succession of publicans. The year Walter Craig died, the Ballarat *Punch* advised its readers that an excellent way to while away a few hours was to go to the morning room at Craig's, call for the papers, a glass of water, and a biscuit. Service would be prompt, and it would be a most economical manner in which to kill time!

Adam Lindsay Gordon, the poet, conducted a livery stables in what is now Craig's yard during the 1860s. His house, which was moved to the Ballarat Gardens in the 1930s, was also there. Gordon was a member of the Ballarat Troop of Light Horse, which drilled behind the hotel, and he could often be seen arriving late from some out-of-town assignment, racing along Lydiard Street on his horse, Maude, leaping off her, and taking his place in the drill line.

Gordon became a tragic figure. His daughter died, and later he suffered a severe head injury when a horse threw him against a wall. He became melancholic and left the district in 1868. Later he committed suicide in Melbourne.

Craig's today has been undergoing considerable renovation, but the Erwins are fascinated by the hotel's history and are making sure it retains its original appearance. Mrs Erwin said: "It's so solidly built it is terribly difficult to do anything with. We made plans to alter various parts but discovered that the bluestone walls were so thick we had to abandon those plans and devise others."

The hotel has close associations with Western District pastoral families; many send their children to school in Ballarat. And often the hotel bubbles with happy end-of-term parties, engagements, birthdays, and wedding receptions.

Craig's present-day patrons bustle across a carpeted marble foyer once trod by Mark Twain and Dame Nellie Melba. Upstairs, guests can still sleep in a bed used by one of the midshipmen, Princes George and Albert, when they visited Ballarat in 1881.

The liberal use of bluestone, such as in Craig's, is a feature of Victorian hotels. It came out in blocks in sailing ships as ballast and was eagerly sought by builders. The hotels pictured are among the better examples of bluestone, particularly the Lancefield Road Hotel at Clarkefield. It was built some 110 years ago by the great pioneering Clarke family, and the bluestone stables in the yard are classified "A" by the National Trust; that is, they are to be preserved at all costs.

Uncle of Alice

He leans back and glares like a desert eagle that's been disturbed during its supper, but there's the suspicion of a smile. "These blokes are easy to handle up here," he says, "when I throw 'em out the door I always throw 'em left or right, never straight ahead. I reckon if I threw 'em straight ahead, they'd go through the brick wall opposite, and I'd have to pay for it."

In the saloon bar of the Alice Springs Hotel, Uncle is holding court, to the raucous accompaniment of the Victorian trots on his ever-present transistor radio. In a town like Alice, there has to be a man like Uncle, the boss man whom everyone knows and whose tastes are law.

The barmaid pulls a round of beers. "Uncle's is the one with the large head," she says, "you understand that, don't you? If he doesn't get a large head on his beer, he gets bloody upset."

Uncle is tired and old but he's still the king of Alice. He presides over his 100-room hotel from a metal table in the corner and when he disappears for his afternoon sleep from three to five his presence is still felt, because this is Uncle's pub, and let no one forget it.

Uncle is L. J. R. Underdown, though few of his subjects would know his full name. He talks tough—"Nah, I don't bother to fight anyone these days. I just throw 'em out." His cluster of admirers nod their agreement, for Uncle's left arm jolt is legendary in these parts. But when you're alone with him, he smiles slyly and says: "These clowns think I'm still the man I used to be, but I'm not."

His pub dominates the town the same way he does. From his rooftop balcony, he has an uninterrupted panorama over the town, which has grown around him, and through The Gap to the southern desert. He has an upstairs restaurant called the Top of the Town which would do credit to the finest city hotel. In the hotel's more boisterous days they had a cricket pitch there, but the stumps have been drawn because Uncle thinks it wouldn't do if someone slammed a six into a plate of Buffalo Tournedos Namatjira.

The restaurant windows command a view which tells the full tale of the Territory's social arrangements. To the left, jocular whites frolic in the hotel pool and, to the right, Aborigines sit in their beer garden, known as the Coliseum, because of the fearful combat which has occurred there on occasions.

Uncle was a raw lad in his early twenties when he left Adelaide and came to the desert selling stores to the miners. Soon an opponent undercut him, and he went broke. So he said to his mother, "We'll build a hotel," to which she replied, "You can't build a hotel, you haven't any money."

Undeterred he set about achieving his ends. "There was just me, a black boy, and a dray. I went outside The Gap and built three kilns and dug those bastard lime bricks out of the ground myself from five in the morning until nine at night, and we carried 'em into town on the dray. We built the pub ourselves, just me and that black boy. Those days the population in the 100 square miles around the place was about 300." By 1933 they had finished, but the town was growing so Uncle decided to build a new pub.

In 1946 they tore down the old place and up went the new. And people came from miles around to gawk at the first elevator in the Northern Territory.

"Hell, I had some trouble puttin' up the new pub. One day I went upstairs and I heard the workmen talking instead of getting on with the job. I said, 'I pay you 18/6 an hour to work, so get on with the job, you bastards.'

"Next day the kitchen girl came to me and said, 'They haven't ordered their morning tea.' I went to them and said, 'I hear you don't want your morning tea?'

"One of 'em said, 'Yeah, after the way you talked to us yesterday, we reckon we don't want your bloody morning tea.' I said, 'What I said yesterday still goes, and you'll have your bloody morning tea and like it.' "

And they did, because Uncle had established his reputation for getting his own way some years earlier owing to the truculence of a gentleman who owed him eight pounds. "I asked him for the money, but he was a big pug and he overawed me and told me where to go. It wasn't long before he owed me twenty-eight pounds so I reckoned I ought to get it. So I said to him, 'You owe me twenty-eight quid,' and he said, 'I don't owe you anything,' with a bloody smirk on his face. So I said, 'You're a liar.'

"He threw one punch which missed one ear, and another which missed the other ear.

"I said, 'Oh, don't let's fight' and I made him shake hands and when we were shakin' hands and smilin' I hit him in the guts with my left. He closed and grabbed me, but I belted him again and chucked him into an open barrel and broke both his collar bones."

We wait until a race ends. Then he says: "I'll tell you how I got the name Uncle. There was a bloke named Butch Verve and he sent me a wire: 'Can you give me a score [£100]?'

"So I wired back: 'Australia all out for 277.'

"He wired to me: 'Uncle, I never thought you'd do that to me.' An' that's how I got stuck with the name. That reminds me about old Misty Mill way back in '29. He was out in the desert and he sent me a letter that said, 'Send me something to eat—I don't care how old or dry it is.' So I sent him his account."

An Aboriginal was hovering nearby, and Uncle was on his feet. "Who are you lookin' for?"

"A friend."

"Well, he isn't here." And the Aboriginal was ushered out the door.

The Coliseum (sometimes known as the Bull Pen) became a landmark in the Territory when Uncle was rebuilding the pub in the 1940s. The Aborigines wanted to drink in the new bars. Uncle said: "I told 'em that if they drank in the beer garden, I'd shout for the first two hours. It cost me 575 quid, and they've stayed there ever since."

Uncle is leaving for his siesta. There is a deferential shuffling of chairs. He says: "I'm old and tired now. I want to get rid of the place. It's not like the old days when we had the cricket pitch upstairs. I liked wicket keepin', you know."

The Parmelia

The story goes that Sir Halford Reddish (who lists his chief recreation as "business") was staying at the old Adelphi Hotel in Perth some years ago when he had the following conversation with Charles Court, then Western Australian Minister for Industrial Development:

Reddish: "Why isn't there a top-class hotel in Perth?"

Court: "Why don't you build one?"

So Sir Halford went home to Britain and had a word with the construction tycoon, Sir Robert McAlpine. And they chipped in about $5 million and created the Parmelia, a truly beautiful grand hotel. The Parmelia opened on 15 December 1968. The chef, Bob Williams, a charming Welshman, recalled: "That day we served breakfast in the Adelphi and lunch in the Parmelia." Then they tore the Adelphi down.

The Parmelia inevitably invites comparison with the Wentworth in Sydney. But the Parmelia people are quietly confident that their hotel is superior. The general manager, Ralph Voigt, said: "The Parmelia is the only hotel in Australia ranking with the best in the world." And the late John Gunther, author of the "Inside" books, said it was the equal of the Ritz in Paris and Claridges in London. It stands in off-white splendour in Mill Street, just down from St George's Terrace, and commands a magnificent view over the Swan.

The Parmelia is not a swingers' hotel; the people who can afford to stay there aren't the type. The visitor enters the foyer to a chorus of "Good morning, sir,"

and the page boys in their traditional pill-box hats appear absolutely crestfallen if any patron succeeds in opening the door before they do. Two Sidney Nolan originals, "Figure and Camels" and "Mother and Child," are tucked away unobtrusively on a wall to the right of the reception area. They're worth perhaps $3,000 each, but to question the Parmelia people about the value of their *objets d'art* would seem positively vulgar. Fine works are scattered almost carelessly about the hotel's ten floors. On a first floor landing, there's a huge, ornate Pier Mirror from Benito Mussolini's palace in Rome.

The hotel was named after the vessel, *Parmelia,* which brought the first settlers to Perth. Today, the hull of that ship would fit inside the hotel ballroom. The

Ralph Voight, general manager of the Parmelia Hotel

hotel originally had 161 rooms, but extensions have increased the number by 200 (tossing in, as well, a pool with a waterfall to the piazza below—nothing pretentious, mind you).

The price of a room for the night starts at twenty-one dollars a single, moving up to twenty-seven dollars for a view of the river, and finally, around $125 a night for a sumptuous penthouse suite on the tenth floor. A British industrialist and his wife occupied the top suite for five months, running up a bill for $20,000 which he paid with a weekly cheque of $1,000. Admiral John McCain, Commander of U.S. Naval Forces in the Pacific, used the hotel as his headquarters for several days in May 1971 and made one request. Could he have access to the roof for his morning skipping? Certainly, they said. The car maker, Henry Ford, hired two whole floors for two days at $1,200 a day, but decided he wanted to stay near the ocean. So the suites were unoccupied, but the bills were paid. One man asked if he could have one and a half pillows. One pillow, he explained, was not quite enough, but two were just too much. He's a regular guest, and whenever he makes a booking, they simply empty half the feathers from one pillow.

No two rooms are furnished alike; there are, in fact, "ladies' rooms" with gentle fabric wallpapers, and far more masculine "men's rooms." And the honeymoon suites! The beds are seven feet square, claimed to be the largest in the Southern Hemisphere, and they are sufficiently large for the timid bride to find a corner to hide or the more enthusiastic couple to romp to their hearts' content! A complimentary bottle of champagne and the Cupid statuary assist to set the mood for such activities. And a discreet curtain divides the gigantic bed from the rest of the suite and thus conceals the bride's blushes from the breakfast waitress.

Breakfast is, indeed, an experience at the Parmelia. Having decided that toast would become cold between the kitchen and the rooms, the management installed a toaster in each room into which the waitress pops the bread with the query: "Light, medium, or dark, sir?" Then to the bathroom with its individual towelling robes and Atkinson's Gold Medal Eau de Cologne soap, imported from Britain. Many guests become so enamoured of the soap that they try to buy some before they leave. (And others become so much more enamoured of the white towelling gowns that they pinch them! The hotel turns away with a discreet cough.)

In the kitchen, Chef Williams has overcome a minor crisis. He received word that there was likely to be a shortage of Russian caviar. "The level of the Caspian Sea's dropping," he explained, "and the sturgeon are diminishing in numbers. You do know how they get the eggs, don't you? Well, it's a sort of round fish, and they catch it and gently stroke the soft underbelly until the eggs come out. Then the fish swims away unharmed. But getting back to the shortage, they're starting to fish the sturgeon for food, as well. Anyhow, I've overcome that by buying 1,000 pounds, just in case."

The caviar will be snapped up in the restaurants for a mere twenty-one dollars for a little more than an ounce—which means that somewhere in the Parmelia, there's stored a king's ransom in Russian caviar, about $300,000 worth.

Chef Williams and his staff of fifty guarantee that no matter what part of the world a guest comes from, they will be able to produce his national dish. "We've never failed yet, but perhaps the strongest challenge came from an American

Bob Williams, Welsh chef of the Parmelia

woman who ordered succotash. We didn't have a clue what it was, but somewhere among our 6,000 recipes we found it—potatoes, carrots, Yippee beans, all mashed together, and fried in a pan. Very tricky, it was!"

The Parmelia is, perhaps, a by-product of the Western Australian mineral boom (menus are printed in Japanese) so it was fitting that much of the Australian production, *The Nickel Queen,* starring Googie Withers, was filmed in the hotel. A boardroom scene was made in the hotel's Waterford Room, an intimate dining room, where the lights from a late eighteenth-century French chandelier and a pair of Waterford candelabra (*circa* 1840) glitter on the gold dinner service.

Even when it is filled to capacity, the Parmelia is strangely quiet. On a typical evening, you would find journalists drinking in Paddy's Find (named after Paddy Hannan who discovered gold at Kalgoorlie); and a gay but nevertheless subdued crowd in the Conference Bar, adjoining perhaps the busiest place of all, the Steak House. In the tasting room behind the bottle shop, a connoisseur might be quietly convincing himself he needs perhaps a few more bottles of Cabernet Sauvignon. An elegant young couple could be sitting in the first floor bar, off the Terrace Restaurant, lazily grilling small steaks on a small charcoal barbecue on the bar.

Many people consider the general manager, Ralph Voigt, to be the leading publican (if that's the correct term!) in Australia. Now in his forties, he came to Australia from Switzerland in 1955. He was an honours graduate from L'Ecole Hotelier, Lausanne. But that meant little in Sydney where he spent his first night sleeping on a billiard table in a crowded pub. He began the slow climb up the hotel ladder—yardman at a Riverina pub, assistant manager of the Menzies, Melbourne, general manager of the Menzies, and now the plum, the Parmelia.

To derive the greatest joy from the Parmelia, one should really spend a few weeks in the outback before plunging into its opulence.

It seems that the ultimate in hotel luxury would be to stand on the balcony of the best penthouse, idly tossing handfuls of caviar to the passing birds.

One of the masterpieces of art at the Parmelia

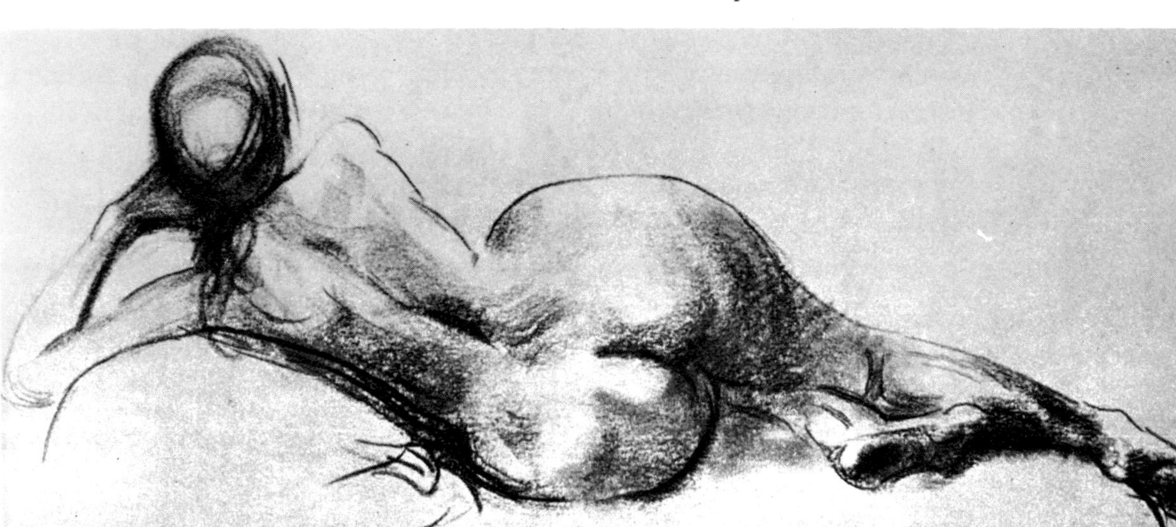

The fancy dress ball

On Saturday, 8 April 1972, a social event of such importance happened in Tennant Creek that the publican was moved to roar the instruction:

"No dogs allowed in the lounge tonight unless they can walk on two legs!"

It was a stinker of a night in the Dead Heart. Flying ants arrived by the ton—and the size of them! You know the length of an ordinary bull-ant? Well, that was the distance between the eyes of those pesky jokers. In the public bar, there was so much slapping of insects off hairy chests that it sounded like an all-in brawl. And there was very nearly a fight around the pool table when a rigger from the new smelter claimed a foul when a Stink Beetle settled on the white ball and rode it into the centre pocket.

But returning to the social event: the Tennant Creek Theatrical Club (Incorporated) had interrupted rehearsals of *Who's Afraid of Virginia Woolf?* to hold a Fancy Dress Ball.

It wasn't frightfully well patronised (Tennant Creek being a, well, fairly crude desert mining town on the road between Alice Springs and Darwin). As Frank Talen, who came as a Red Indian, explained: "The miners think theatricals are poofters."

Nevertheless, those that came did the town proud. There was one Ned Kelly, six Indians, two chaps in their wives' old frocks, and one bloke who came as a drunken mechanic in greasy overalls and had a great time until they discovered he wasn't in fancy dress at all. Jan, the barmaid, who smiled a lot, turned up without

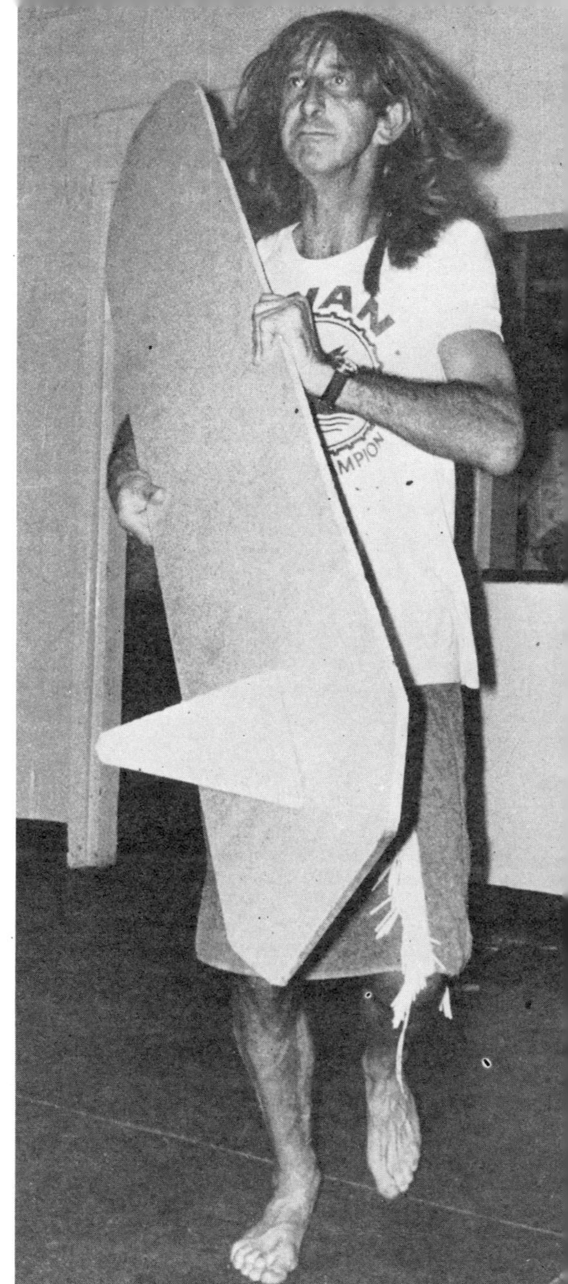

a bra and a wit yelled: "Hey, anyone got a lacrosse net to stop her tits hitting the floor?" Raucous laughter followed that!

The power failed twice, and someone placed a clammy hand on a woman's thigh, so she shrieked: "Well, at least it's my husband." And a gruff voice replied: "Do ya wanna bet?"

They held the ball in the dining room at the Tennant Creek pub with a band composed of three electric guitarists and a chap on the drums. Of course, every

time the power failed so did the electric guitars, and there was much learned discussion about this. Someone said: "I reckon, personally speaking, that there's too much of a drain on the power. I mean, it's the first time we've ever had three electric guitars going in Tennant Creek at once, isn't it?"

It was generally agreed that the fancy dress parade was the best part. Frank Talen won the single section but he couldn't attend the presentation because he was getting a jug of beer, and everyone understood that was far more important.

A local identity of some note named Dapper Dan the Cemetery Man tried to enter on the grounds that he had the only tie in Tennant Creek, but he was rejected for being facetious. There was another Dan who threw out a strong challenge to Frank—Dan the Karate Man. He tossed himself vigorously around the floor, somersault after somersault, until finally he slammed against a pillar, and the whole pub shook. So he was disqualified for a breach of etiquette.

Bob Christie, the publican, appeared as Murph the Surfie, wearing a Swan

Brewery shirt and Jan's wig. With a cry of "Surf's up!" he hurled himself onto his board, skidded across the concrete floor, and narrowly avoided the total dismantlement of his manhood. One young fellow made an entrance from the public bar carrying his mate over his shoulders.

"What do you represent?" the judges asked.

"Huh?"

"What have you come as?"

"Nothin'. I'm just trying to carry my cobber to the dunny before he chunders."

They made way with alacrity.

A gentleman, who came as a woman in a fine feathered hat, sheer dress, and high heels, gave an exclusive interview to the press (now to be published for the first time):

"On me way here, I thought I'd drop into the Goldfields Hotel for a beer to build up courage. Anyhow, I needed a piss so I went to the gents—and they all tried to rape me! So I went to the ladies, and they all screamed, so finally I had to piss under a tree outside."

Regretfully, there was something of a shortage of young ladies. When a barmaid began canoodling with her boyfriend, Bob Christie ordered her to desist.

"When the other blokes who haven't got birds see something like that, they get steamed up and start to fight each other," he explained.

As it was, many of the young dears had been seduced away to a corner by Old What's 'Is Name, who came down from Darwin. He'd drawn them into a corner to relate tales which caused their little bosoms to rise and fall and their lips to breathe: "Gee whizz."

He was saying: "Yeah, I was out on the river t'other day when I seen this crocodile, see. So I thought, 'I'll 'ave this one.' So I shoots him fair in the back of the 'ead, and he sinks straight to the bottom.

"He's too good to lose, see, so I thinks, 'I'll have to get 'im' so I strips off and dives in. After a couple of minutes, I spot 'im on the bottom and grab 'im. And there was a Gawd Almighty struggle. I reckon I wrestled with 'im for five minutes before I dragged 'im to the surface still thrashing and finally I chucked him into the boat where I knocked him unconscious. And do you know what? There wasn't a bullet 'ole in 'im. He was the wrong croc."

"Gee whizz!"

Old What's 'Is Name is given another jug.

"Yeah, I'm a fisherman, actually," he said.

"Gee whizz! What sort of boat have you got?"

"Boat? Wadda you mean, boat? I use a horse and dray. I go down to the Elizabeth River and drive the horse and dray in, see. Then I put honey on the horse's tail and, sure enough, all the flies settle on the horse's tail. Well, the fish come up, try to grab the flies, and the horse boots 'em into the dray with his left hind leg. When the dray's full of fish, we go home."

"Gee whizz!"

"Of course," he added, "you've gotta wash the honey off the horse's tail before you go home or the flies can be murder."

"Gee whizz!"

"Yeah, I was out the other day fishin' with a line when I hooked this bloody big barramundi. He walked me two miles down the river before he came up against a fence through the stream dividin' two stations. I tried to pull 'im ashore, but he was about as big as a pig and I couldn't. So I went to get the horse and dray to haul 'im out.

"Anyhow, when I got back, he'd gone, and he'd dragged the fence with him. And not only that, he'd taken fourteen miles of fences with him. It cost me a pretty penny to replace them fences, I'm telling you."

The gay crowd are consuming great amounts of sparkling star wine. Frank Talen said: "The pseudo-sophisticates drink beer—out of the bottle."

The conversation is theatrical: "I do wish we could encourage more people to attend our premieres—one hundred is just not good enough."

"We asked the miners what they'd like."

"Oh, yes, and what do they want?"

"They said they'd like some Shakespeare so we're putting on *Twelfth Night* in October."

"Oh, darling, you don't think they're putting you on, do you?"

Two in the morning, and they trickle into the desert night. And a jolly good time was had by all.

The pub with the big backyard

It's only a small pub, the Wauchope Well Hotel. But what a backyard—2,000 square miles!

The thirsty traveller knows he's approaching a watering hole when his car thumps over a cattle grid bearing the sign: "Singleton Station." Nineteen miles later, the pub appears as a lonely speck in an endless desert of scrub, sand, and stones. From the shady verandah, there is an uninterrupted view of nothing 400 miles west to the Western Australian border and beyond. No human lives there—the ghost gums reign supreme.

The publican is Malcolm Roberts, who holds the lease on the 2,000-square-mile Singleton Station. At one time he was just a cattleman but one day he decided to take over the pub which bordered his land. He is weary of jokes like: "Lucky you didn't put the toilets right down the back. Ha, ha."

In his bar, dust-begrimed road train drivers quaff their beer beside genteel lady tourists from the south eating ice cream. Once they depart and drive north, they will still be in the pub yard until they reach the spectacular rocks known as the Devil's Marbles, ten miles north.

The Roberts have a homestead some miles from the pub but they spend much of their time at the hotel. So the Wauchope Well must be one of the few hotels which doubles as a station homestead.

CITY MOTELS
BAR

The playboy

The In Crowd call him Pal, this smooth, if aging, groover. In his white Daimler, he tears down from his rag shop in town to his pub by the sea. Jonathon Crawford is in his early forties, still rated an eligible bachelor by the Toorak society mums. He is a dress designer with a flair for running pubs—in particular, his Pacific Hotel in the south Victorian coastal resort of Lorne. During the week he's to be found in his rag shop in Flinders Lane where the decor seems to consist solely of vast blow-ups of newspaper articles flattering to Jonathon Crawford. But at the weekend, Crawford the designer becomes Crawford the jovial country publican dispensing largesse in the unashamedly-named Jet Set Bar where he conducts fast conversation with his social-circuit cronies from town and the Western District; he is tastefully attired in elastic-sided boots, the badge of their affluence. And when the bars close, Crawford retires to his bachelor nest above the town, away from the pub, where he conducts what he terms his "late late show."

The Pacific Hotel was built in the 1880s, and Crawford took it over in the early 1960s. "I was a surfie down there when I was a kid of about eighteen. I had my eye on the pub then. All my mates said, 'You'll own it one day, pal,' and it just seemed natural that I should buy it. Anyway, I was spending all my dough there and I reckoned I ought to get some value for it." He did have some early problems; it used to be known as the College of Carnal Knowledge owing to

the nature of its clientele, but he eventually managed to get rid of them. Now the Porches and Volvos cram the car park in front of the pub. "It's a pub for the twenty to thirty-five age group," he said. "I have a fit—or nearly—when someone over forty comes in. I can't see how they'd enjoy it." His great gimmick out of season is his Weekend for Swinging Singles. It's a very sexy pub.

"I've seen that many guys coming down the stairs with someone else's wife I don't even notice. I just don't want to know, man. I play it straight around the pub. I've got to set the example. I don't single out any particular chick because the others might get upset."

Without prompting, Crawford will relate the tale of how he came to purchase the hotel: "I used to bring all my friends down from Melbourne, and that particular year was a vivid one, because I had 400 coming to dinner on Saturday night and I wanted the food to be good, but it was bloody awful—rabbit instead of chicken. So I said to Ron Todd, the publican, 'Look Toddy, you've just got to get it right. You'll send me out of my mind! No one will ever talk to me again.'

"So Toddy said, 'Look, Jon, I'd like to sell the bloody place to you,' and that's how it happened."

Crawford wonders now whether he has outlived his usefulness at the Pacific. "Maybe it needs a new image," he mused. "I might get out—buy another pub. I'm in my forties now. I'll have to slow down one of these days."

The Babbo boys, local sawmillers, in the public bar of the Pacific

The Continental

There could hardly have been a more Australian pub than the old tin Continental at Broome. A great, ugly edifice but oh, so charming. One day they decided it had lived too long.

So they began to build a smart new pub behind it, but they used their imagination—the interior decorators came from Perth and sat in the old bars to absorb the atmosphere. And finally they created a new pub which looked almost as ancient as the original.

In a country where so many old places are being ruthlessly destroyed, it is a refreshing sight.

THE CONTINENTAL
HOTEL

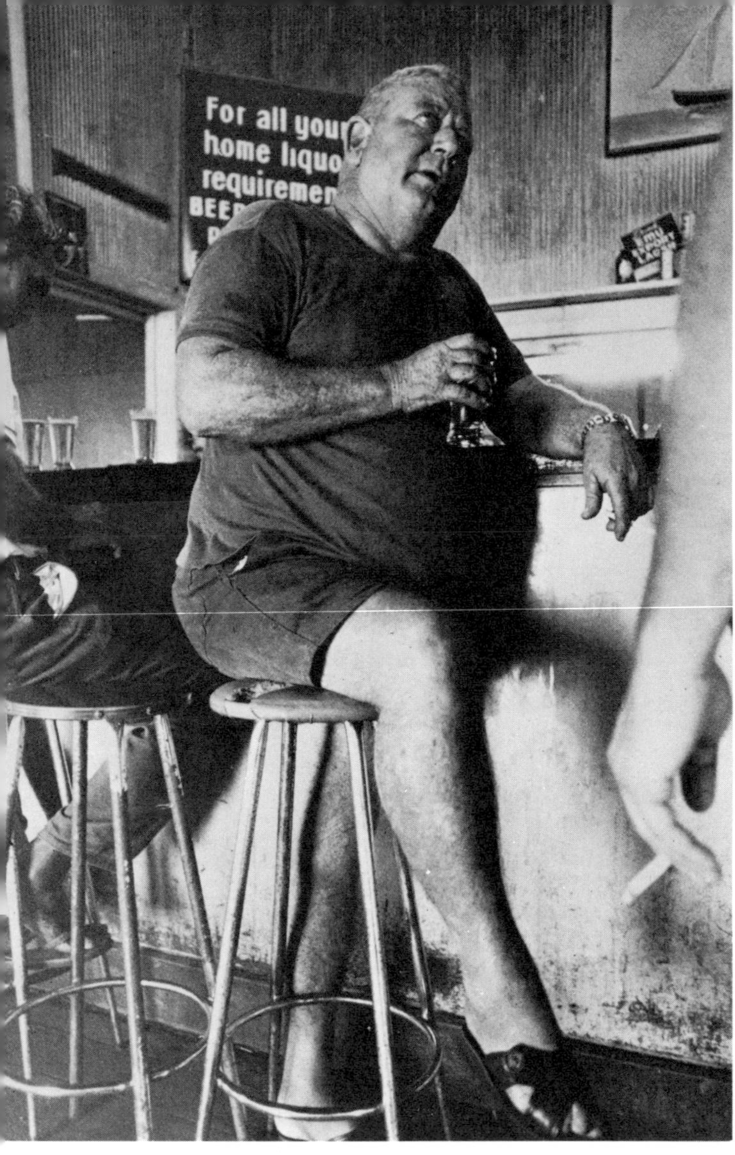

Personalities at the Continental Hotel, Broome

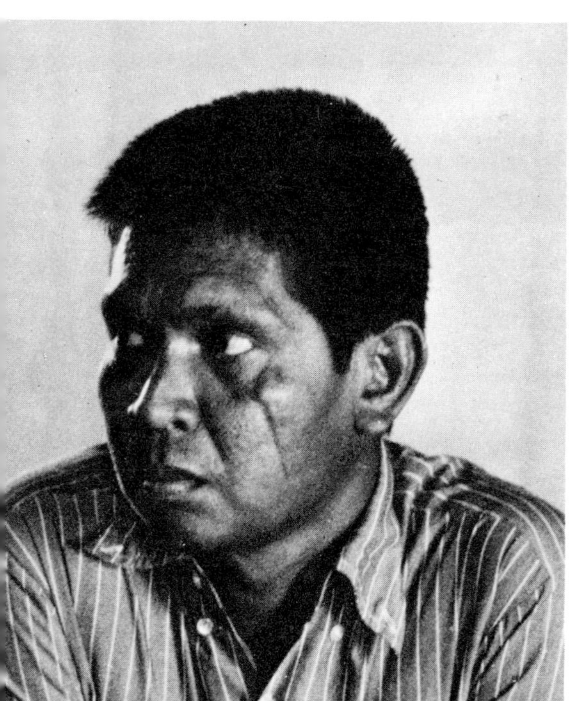

Ginty

Ginty was in his late sixties, a leprechaun of a man, barely five feet tall. But he was a big, big man in the pub at Bajool, on the railway line south of Rockhampton. On the wall of the pub, there was a photograph of two emus drawing a sulky. Ginty's emus.

"I believe I am," he said, "the first man in Australia to train emus to draw his cart around the place." Few would argue with that!

Ginty (real name: Jim Offord) was standing in the yard outside the pub and getting the feel of a large stockwhip, while several drinkers watched him from the doorway. Ten paces away his pup, Jack, sat patiently, smoking a cigarette at the end of a long holder.

"Right, boy!" said Ginty.

Crack!

He deftly flicked the cigarette from Jack's mouth with the stockwhip. Everyone cheered, and they set up another beer for Ginty.

It's not every pub that can boast a man like Ginty. His house was a short emu's gallop from the pub and it was a sight to warm the heart of a brewery baron; the doors, walls, and window frames were decorated with the tops of beer bottles; hundreds of them. Even Jack's collar had its quota.

"It's been my hobby," he said, "collected 'em for years. A daughter of mine's a barmaid in Rockhampton." His pride shone through.

"I was in the railways for twenty-seven years but before that I was a jockey and I always had a love for animals. I couldn't hurt anything. Anyway, about ten years ago, I bet a bloke I could harness two emus to a gig. I got a bloke to

look out for some emus for me, and one day he sent me these two chicks—their mother had been killed. So I sent him two quid. Oh, it didn't take long for me to train 'em to the harness and, crikey, they could move. We were getting about town at up to thirty-five miles an hour, y'know. One day one of 'em stuck his head through the wire around their paddock and choked himself, and the other one just refused to pull the gig any more.. I'm the only person who can go near him now. That pup's the same. He's only seven months old but he knows I wouldn't cut him with the stockwhip. If I've had a few beers, I just give him a longer cigarette holder, just to make sure."

Jim Buckley's

"A kid of fourteen painted a couple of trees on the way home from school, came here, and stuck the picture on the wall in the pub. It was there for months. He came in every day. 'Have you sold my painting yet?' Anyway, one day we were hosing the bar and splashed it with water and, being a watercolour, it ran. We were at our wits' end; we didn't know what to tell him. Anyway, he came in next day and said 'Where's my painting?' so I said, 'We sold it for five quid.' I gave him the fiver, and his eyes lit up. I suppose he thought he'd made it; he'd sold a picture in Jim Buckley's pub."

This was the gentle Jim Buckley, talking through a friend; he had undergone a throat operation, and normal speech was no longer possible. When we visited Jim Buckley's Newcastle Hotel in George Street, Sydney, it was under a death sentence, having to make way for the huge Rocks development. It was a pub that would be sadly missed, a cosy corner in a hard, bustling city. Scores of paintings lined the walls—in the back bar, only the inevitable "Gents" sign broke the row of pictures. A tough part of the city, not far from the docks, but the crowd was quiet and the barmaids were pretty.

A majestic nude dominated one wall; this was Jim's own picture. She was a Dutch girl and once she adorned the wall of the Sergeants' Mess at the North Head army barracks. But when the wives objected, the picture was moved to Buckley's. The faithful at Jim's pub believe she is greater than Chloe, the beautiful nude at Young and Jackson's in Melbourne. Jim Orme, who managed

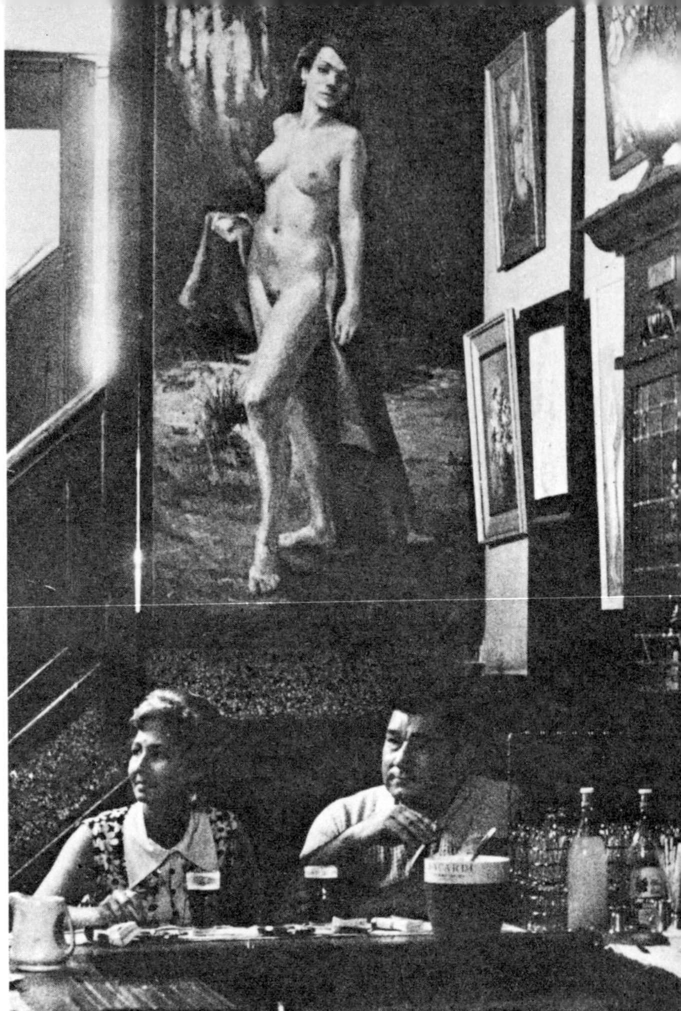

the Newcastle for Jim Buckley, said: "Chloe's not really a nude. She's wearing a bangle on her left wrist."

That, most assuredly, would be fighting talk in Melbourne!

In fact, they displayed their scorn of Chloe at Buckley's by pasting a cheap copy of the painting behind a clock in the public bar. "We had an exhibition here once," Jim said, "and at least twenty of the nudes would have left Chloe for dead."

Anyone could display a painting at the Newcastle. "The artists have to put fair commissions on their work, and when we sell a picture for them, we pass the commission on to the Spastic Centre. Paintings have sold here from a few bob up to $2,000," Jim said.

Jim Buckley is a millionaire, so he could afford to smile over the $30,000 in dud cheques he had pasted to boards in an upstairs room at the pub.

Every so often, they'd bring the cheques down and hold an exhibition of them.

It made a nice change.

Opal Inn, Coober Pedy

The stars vie for glory in the black velvet desert night and the monstrous moon glows on the heaps of rejected earth. And in the lounge bar of the Opal Inn, two men mutter words which smack of equally monstrous sums of money.

"Come now, sir, what have you got?" says the handsome Farid Khan, the Pakistani from Hong Kong.

Behind him lurks the faithful Abdullah Chan, a smiling Buddha. It's said that Abdullah is Farid's bodyguard, a man with a fierce karate chop, an image the wily Farid tends to nurture, for there are many men of uncertain character abroad in this tough little town.

"Umm, what have you got?" says the opal miner. He is fencing, and none

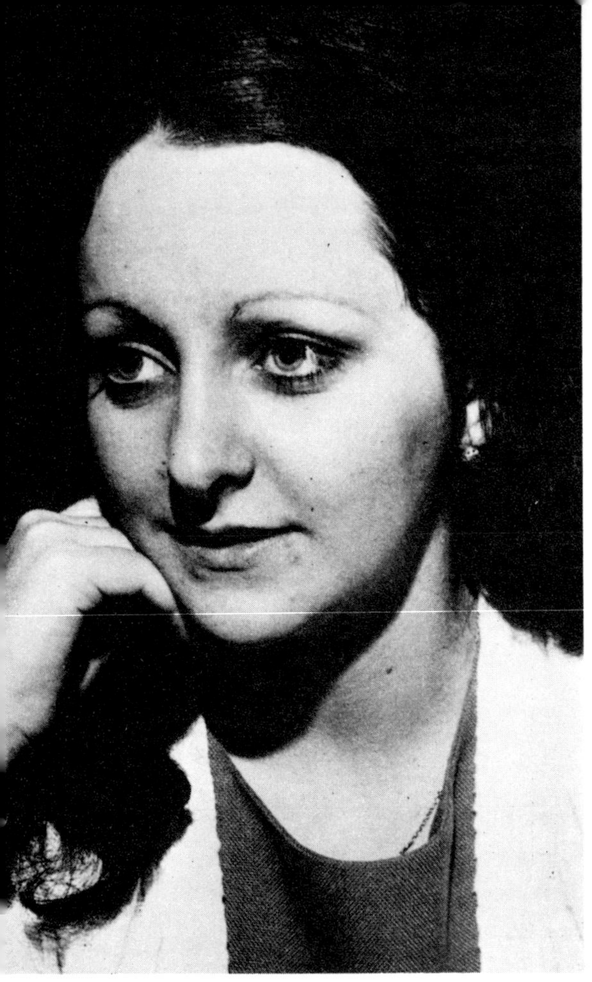

knows better than the astute Farid Khan. He twirls his black moustache in anticipation of the pleasurable haggling which must surely follow.

"Come, come, sir," says Farid. And the miners around him, their bodies permanently ingrained with sand, suck their schooners and pretend not to hear. But oh, their ears are flapping!

"I've got a good parcel of grey opal," says the miner, and he is whispering nervously.

"Please, come to my dugout tomorrow," says Farid, and the man drifts away.

The other buyers have been watching. They try to catch the miner's eye, but he is well satisfied, because it is known that the Pakistani pays a fair price. And it's also known that he has a good market in West Germany for grey opal. Farid takes us to his dugout down the main street. A four-wheel drive truck passes, tossing up a great cloud of dust, and for several minutes the stars are obscured.

Like most other residents of Coober Pedy, the world's greatest opal centre, Farid and Abdullah live underground. Three doors, one of steel mesh, guard their treasure house. Their home is opulent—seagrass matting on the floors, glittering white stone walls, a vinyl topped bar; there are rooms and more rooms carved from the earth.

Farid shows us the workroom where Abdullah cuts and polishes the opals ("He's not really a bodyguard—he couldn't hurt a fly," Farid says). And in a cave off the workroom, where a safe has been thrust into the wall, lies the result of Farid's wheeling and dealing in the bar at the Opal Inn: bags and bags of uncut stones.

"Oh, there'd be about $35,000 worth here, I imagine," Farid says, carelessly. But he's not really so careless, as the bars across the ventilation hatches testify.

The less permanent buyers live in a row of ground floor rooms at the pub. There are cards on their doors: "Opal Buyer, M. Schumann," "Wong Ying Kwai, Opal Buyer." Farid once lived in the hotel until an unfortunate event occurred.

"I went to sleep one night after chaining my canvas bag of opal, about $18,000 worth, to a leg of my bed. Now, I usually sleep on my side but this night I fell asleep on my back and I was very restless. I awoke, and a big man was standing in the darkness like a ghost with a stocking over his head.

"I had an iron bar beside me in case of such a happening but, like a bloody idiot, I grabbed my torch and shone it in his face. I jumped up and next I felt the knife running down my throat. I knocked him down, but he ran off.

"Now, I wish to be fair about this. I'm not sure he intended to stab me—perhaps he only wanted to cut the opal bag loose. Anyway, the gentleman who tried to rob me is still here." We agreed, somewhat nervously, not to go any further into the matter. The Flying Doctor took Farid to Port Augusta where he was patched up, and he continued his wheeling and dealing.

Anna Coro, teenage daughter of the Opal Inn's licensee, Bob Coro, said: "Nowadays, the nine rooms used by the buyers have their own safes, each with its own combination."

The Opal Inn is a splendid stone monolith in the flat town, and the brewery sign on its roof beckons the dry-throated miners from miles around. The lounge bar would do justice to any city hotel, but there is something missing: girls. The miners sit in silent groups and gaze longingly at the odd female who swishes

Facing page: LEFT: Anna Coro, daughter of the Opal Inn's licensee, Bob Coro
RIGHT: Farid's uncut opals

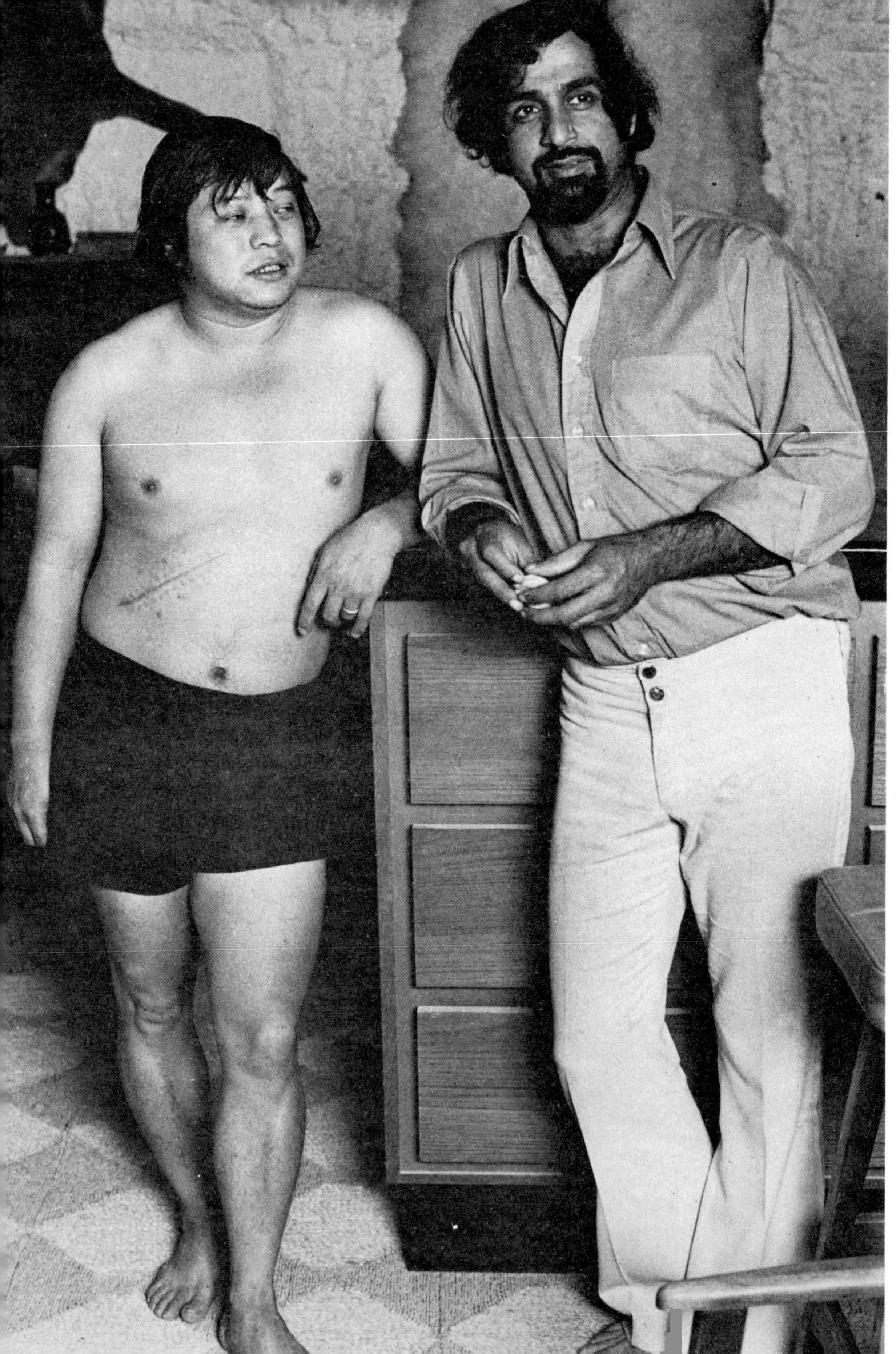

past. Some, no doubt, would love to leave Coober Pedy for ever but they are trapped in the settlement. Anna said: "They come here with enough money to get started in their mines, but soon it's all gone. They start buying everything on credit from the stores and before long they are so deeply in debt they cannot leave."

A tourist bus towing a trailer carrying the passengers' tents stops outside, and suddenly the bar is bursting with women, girls in their mid-twenties. It's as if a whistle has been blown; the miners appear from nowhere, some so dusty it is clear that in their haste they have foregone showers. The girls are bold, laughing loudly and casting tantalising looks around. Eyes meet, the band appears (miners all). It is quite obvious that many of the young ladies have the same thing on their minds as the men, and happiness returns to the Opal Inn.

The pub is good for everyone; for one thing, it is above the ground.

A miner says: "When you're living in a hole in the ground like a rabbit and spending your days scratching around in another hole in the ground, it does something beaut to you to get nice and full above the surface."

The rash old days when a man would toss a handful of stones on the bar to be admired by one and all are gone. Only the negotiations are carried out there; the stones and cash change hands in private.

Anna said: "Sometimes a man will come here and buy champagne to celebrate a great success. Everyone drinks with him but secretly they think it very foolish." She is a remarkable young girl, straight from a convent in Adelaide into the hurly-burly at Coober Pedy. When her father is absent, she runs the pub with the help of thirty staff. A mere slip of a girl but stern enough to make the roughest man quake. To be barred from the pub would be disastrous.

Farid Khan appears, a picture of smiling satisfaction. He has made a good buy: a parcel of fossilised sea shells and snails, each containing a glorious, sea-green opal.

Another miner gestures to him, and soon the muttering has begun again. It is business as usual in the lounge of the Opal Inn.

Facing page: Farid Khan (right), opal buyer, and his bodyguard, Abdullah Chan (left)

The Casino

In 1856 one David Dunkley publicly protested about the stench of whales being dried on the beach beside his house on the banks of Hobart's Derwent River. Today on that very same place, standing stark against the background of Mount Wellington, a gambler's haven beckons.

Even in the sophisticated 1970s it comes as a shock to find that Australia finally has her first casino. And it comes as an even greater shock that it has risen from the ground in conservative Tasmania. The Wrest Point Casino is Tasmania's bold bid to join the jet set; it is a charming island but used to be too far from the well-trodden tourist track. But now, will they be drawn there by the lure of the fast buck, the cry of the croupier? And when the gambler wearies of the tables, he can escape to such places as Port Arthur and wallow in the island's convict past.

Federal Hotels built their casino in front of their Wrest Point Hotel, traditionally the island's main meeting point for businessmen and tourists. It is an eminently respectable casino, supervised by the Tasmanian Government treasury. An eager gambler, having won a pile on the Sydney or Melbourne races, can wing his way to Hobart in an hour or so to try to double it on the tables.

The casino is situated only two miles from Hobart's city centre. The gambling rooms are located on the ground floor of a 230-foot circular tower. On the upper floors there are a 350-seat theatre, all-night grill room, heated swimming pool, sauna baths, shops, all topped by a sumptuous revolving restaurant with magnificent views of the Derwent and the mountains surrounding the city, Australia's southernmost State capital.

There's accommodation for 620 people, and the facilities are such that the truly fanatical gambler need never leave the building.

To ensure a smooth-running casino, Federal Hotels imported Ron Hurley, the young casino manager of the Playboy Club in London. The roulette wheels came from Paris.

Tasmania is poised for a new era of greatness. Who knows? Perhaps Jackie Kennedy, Aristotle Onassis, and their chums will drop by on occasions. One day, even swinging Sydney may take second place to this new Monte Carlo of the south-west Pacific.

Three little posies

Three little posies, all in a row; three little beds, all in a row; and three little bathrobes, all in a row.

The mighty Hotel Australia in Adelaide was awaiting three little girls. Well, not so little, perhaps; sixteen or seventeen, coming to town from their fathers' sheep stations for their exclusive school's end-of-term ball. It would be an evening of nerves and flutters; the hotel understood that and they'd stocked the 'fridge with soft drinks to moisten three dry young throats.

Late in the afternoon the hotel's general manager, J. Henry Ehrlich, a Swiss-Austrian, who has managed such splendid establishments as the Peninsula in Hong Kong, left his ground-floor office to make a final check of the fifty-dollars-per-night suite the girls' fathers had taken for them. "Their fathers have been in touch with us," he smiled. "They asked us to look after them." But that went without saying, for J. Henry Ehrlich is a man for the personal touch. Every day he spends two or three hours in the lobby, talking to guests, shaking their hands, and listening to what they have to say. He prides himself on personally knowing every one of the guests in his 154 rooms within a day of their arrival.

The Wrest Point Casino on the Hobart skyline

Warren and his bar, National Hotel, Brisbane

Facing page:
TOP Suite, The Parmelia, Perth
BOTTOM Seven-foot square honeymoon beds, The Parmelia

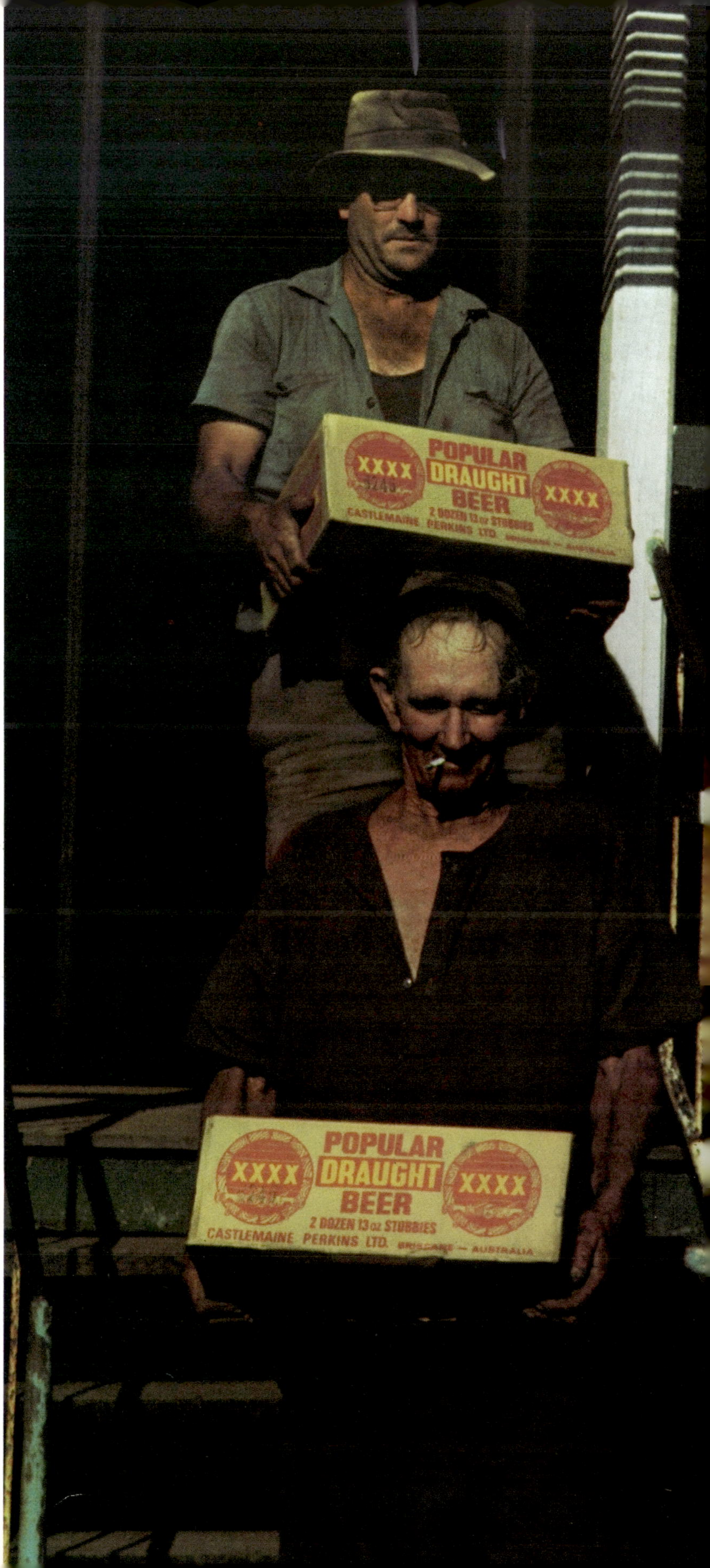

Above: Kingoonya, South Australia

Left: The pub with no walls or doors, Fitzroy Crossing, Western Australia

Right: Saving the beer, Kuttabul, Queensland

Above: Go Go Jack sinks a pot, Fitzroy Crossing
Facing page: Mineshaft Bar, Black Lion Hotel, Broken Hill, New South Wales

Overleaf: The pub the ants built, old Halls Creek, Western Australia

When the old South Australian closed, there was something of a well-mannered struggle among Adelaide's better hotels for its clientele. The Hotel Australia appears to have won. In keeping with most great hotels, the Australia's lobby is invariably quiet, but the peace disguises great activities happening on the floors above. "Our greatest income comes from functions," Ehrlich said, "and we have more facilities for them than any other hotel in Australia. We can accommodate 2,400 people at functions at any one time. Why, there may be five bands playing in the hotel at once."

J. Henry Ehrlich of the Hotel Australia, Adelaide

Ehrlich is a man who looks to the future. His first-floor discotheque is always crowded with the city's youth. He claims to make no profits out of it—but he knows that as they grow older, he will win them over to the Australia. "There are girls who come here and nurse one drink all night," he said, "but one day they will marry and perhaps have their wedding reception in this hotel."

As with most big hotels, Japanese businessmen are an important part of the trade—the Australia gets twenty to thirty a week—so they have imported their own Japanese receptionist, Reiko Omiro, to welcome them. It is not the only Australian hotel to do this, but the Australia claims one thing above all the others: the finest city skyline view in the country.

From the Colonel Light Room (and bedrooms below) there's an unimpeded view of the city lights and the hills beyond.

The Barbary Coast, Cairns

The Barbary Coast has the toughest, most vicious stretch of pubs in the land. It is a haunt for the wanton, the derelict, and the savage. And Kay Fisher, a diminutive, fortyish, Japanese-born mother-of-six, is the Queen of the Barbary Coast. Her pub is the Barrier Reef, a hangout for sullen Aborigines and lonely coloured seamen. The whites spit out its nickname—the Spearthrower's Arms. On the doorway to what passes for a lounge bar, there's a sign which says: "Never a dull moment."

Mrs Fisher shrugged her shoulders: "Someone painted it there. There's so many fights. I reckon I might even advertise it." If you've a fist and nerves of iron, it might be a good place to stay, just two dollars a night, bed and breakfast.

"It's a blacks' pub," she said. "The coloureds hate the whites. They'll all get together to fight a white and they'd kick him to pieces. So I don't let coloureds and whites fight each other. If anyone else wants to fight, I send 'em down to the coconut tree beside the pub. We call it the Fightin' Tree. And I go down to the Fightin' Tree to referee, make sure they don't fight dirty, kick each other,

that sort of thing. I've got to look after my customers. If I want 'em to stop fighting, I scream 'Stop!' and they stop. Most of the fighting's over girls. These coloured girls in here aren't prostitutes, they're not like that. They say, 'I love this fella, I'll go with him.' It's free love, you know."

At noon, last night's contraceptives still lay on the pavement outside.

The pubs on the Barbary Coast stand side by side opposite the wharves; they are homes for broken old men, lying in their crude beds on upstairs verandahs and not the least bit interested in leaving their grubby sheets.

The feeling of hopelessness is overwhelming.

Kuttabul, central Queensland coast

The fire was growing wilder in the south, and they feared it might sweep the pub away. Oh, tragedy! So they started moving the beer out—just in case. The publican, Harry Denham, helped them wheel it to the utility trucks, having thoughtfully suggested they might like to pay in the event of it not finding its way back to the pub.

But, we are happy to report, the pub didn't burn down.

And those poor fire-fighters had to drink all that beer. Oh, damn! It's a hard life.

The fire-fighters, Kuttabul, Queensland

The Mitre

Ye Olde Mitre Tavern is a charming inn, very much in the English style, yet incongruously tucked away, like a doll's house, among Melbourne's tall towers of commerce. When the office workers come down to earth, they can transport themselves instantly into the Dickensian era, simply by entering the Mitre.

In August 1930 a journalist, R. W. E. Wilmot, wrote an article in the *Argus* about the old tavern. His piece was obviously a labour of love, and it would be impossible for anyone to give a better impression of what the Mitre meant:

"No hotel in Australia is quite like the Mitre Tavern, in Bank Place, Melbourne. In all the years I have known it, it has never changed. Other hotels have been rebuilt or renovated, but the Mitre is as it always has been. You go into the little bar parlour through a low door under the staircase. The doorway is so narrow that there is room only to admit the entry of one person at a time and then not a giant. The building is of two stories, surrounded on two sides by lanes. The front is upon Bank Place, and the back nestles under the high walls of Temple Court. It reminds one forcibly of some of the little hotels in Fleet Street, London.

"Its history is crowded with reminiscence. It has filled a place in the life of the west end of the city for more than half a century. Mr George Ross Fenner, who speaks with personal knowledge of the establishment of the Atheneum and the Victoria Amateur Turf Club, can tell of habitués of the Mitre away back in the seventies. He talks of the Dog Club, which met there more than

sixty years ago. He recalls intimately such well-known coursing and racing men who gathered there as the Whittingham brothers, John Wagner, C. B. Fisher and his brother Hurtle, A. W. Robertson, Arthur Blackwood, Tom Haydon, who was the licensee and was succeeded by H. Greville, the caterer, and George Watson, the prince of starters.

"What a wonderful hunting family the Watsons were! Mr George Watson was master of the Melbourne until he handed over his whip to his son, Godfrey; and, says Mr Fenner, 'at one and the same time, while George Watson was master of the Melbourne, his brother, Robert, was master of the Carlo in Ireland, and another brother, William, was master of the Cotswold in England, and his grandfather and father had been masters of the Carlo before that. His nephew, John, was master of the Meath, in Ireland.' Mr Fenner added: 'I shall never forget George Watson. I bought several hunters from him, and he never sold me a bad one and never charged me full price.'

"Hunting and coursing men made the Mitre their headquarters in those days. There the first polo club, established in Victoria in 1874, held its meetings under the presidency of Sir Redmond Barry [who sent Ned Kelly to the gallows]. Captain Standish was vice-president, and the committee included such well-known men as Robert Power, Reginald Bright, Finlay Campbell, Edward Fanning, and Herbert Power.

"Membership extended far and wide, and the club had many of the members at its headquarters in the Mitre; they included Hastings Cunningham, James Grice, James Graham, Alex Landale, Herbert Henty, Hickman and Robert Molesworth, and Robert and Colin Simson.

"Later the Mitre became the rendezvous of lawyers and businessmen associated with the law. It was only a step from Temple Court and from Chancery Lane. Selbourne Chambers had not yet been built. Sir Bryan O'Loghlen had his office in Temple Court, later occupied by Charles Miller. J. L. Purves, K.C.—The Emperor they called him—and his right-hand man, Walter Coldham, were regular patrons. There were many who can recall J.L. telling some of his stories to a little crowd of admirers around him.

"With him would be some of the pigeon-shooting men such as William Sayers and Bill Gannon (from Sydney). The Dalgety staff took lunch there and each would be given his luncheon free. The staff used to lunch in the office but later it lunched at the office's expense. Each Monday morning, everyone was supplied with five luncheon tickets—funny little parchments they were—which entitled the holder to luncheon at the Mitre or at the Mia Mia, the first of Melbourne's tea-rooms.

"Day by day, one could see W. G. Watson, the manager; Edward Simmonds, the accountant, who was for so many years a member of the Liedertafel Choir; George Simpson, manager of the produce department; Harry Wood; Harry Brush, the cashier of the wool department; Charles Bucknill, manager of the bond, in top-hat and frocked coat; and his boon companion, Edward Kenny; Joseph Woolf McCheane, who had the reputation of having fished more and caught less than any other man in Melbourne; J. T. Cosgrove, manager of the shipping department, and secretary of the charting firm of Blackwood, Knox and Brown; T. S. Huggins, who recently retired from the secretaryship of the Royal Melbourne Golf Club; J. T. P. O'Meara, now secretary of the Honorary Justices Association; A. G. Leeds, later manager in Perth; Frank Guthrie, later manager at Geelong; David Luke; Tom Borwick; C. E. Howard, afterwards manager of the Melbourne office; George L. Aitken, the present manager; George Officer, Harry Ford, Joe Hallows, W. P. Whitney, still cashier; Tom Cochrane, and so many more. The Mitre was and is a great Dalgety house, for the system of issuing luncheon tickets to the staff still prevails.

"There was one little coterie which one could always be sure to see some time in the day, usually in the morning—Thomas Bent, then Speaker, but later Sir Thomas, the Premier; with J. F. Hamilton, H. H. Budd, Arthur Walstab, and W. Park, of the Colonial Mutual Insurance Company, and occasionally A. E. Clarke, especially if there were anything to be done for the East Melbourne Cricket Club. With them, one would often see David Gaunson. I wonder how often he played the piano in the old parlour, standing up, and with him, his right-hand man, John Cullen. Another politician often noted was Joseph Tilley Brown, who represented a constituency in the north-east of the State, and was also in the Federal Parliament, and I recall Cornelius Bannister, in a grey bell-topper, a morning coat, and black tie, followed by two cocker spaniels which never seemed to leave him. A little athletic man, with his hat tilted to one side, he always looked like a Dickensian character. J. G. Pearson, the wine and spirit merchant, sportsman, and athlete, is also recalled.

"Other names and faces flit across my memory—Hugh Montmorency, from the Trustees Executors' Company, and his brother, Jim, who established a tea agency in Temple Court; O'Hara Wood, the barrister; Fred Neave, W. H. Woolcott, and Harry Graves, the solicitors; W. W. Gaggin, the cricketer, fisherman, and field game shot; Robert John de Courcy Talbot who lunched there day by day with Hector McDonald, and Smith McDonald, the land valuer; Fred Saunders, one of the founders of the Savage Club, which has its quarters in Bank Place nowadays; Sir Rupert Clarke, who had his flat nearby; Arthur Harston, and his partner, George Partridge, the law stationers; Scobie Gair; William Jardine, the Irish solicitor, who used to drive a jaunting car."

What a marvellous picture Wilmot conjures up! Imagine being trapped in that Dalgety school. And isn't it intriguing to know where old Tommy Bent, whose statue stands in Brighton, got his splendid pot belly! It is almost unbelievable that hunters and their hounds set forth from the Mitre with the cry, "Hark, forward! Hark, forward! Tanting!" Today they would be swallowed in the concrete canyons.

A pioneer, Charles Hotson Ebden, bought the land on which the Mitre stands on 1 June 1837, just two years after the first settlers landed at Melbourne and bought it from the Aborigines for assorted tomahawks, knives, and other implements. Ebden paid £136 for the land—and only thirty-nine years later, it was worth £73,000 an acre. Tradition has it that the building was originally a private residence, then Government offices. In 1869 Henry Thompson successfully applied for the first licence.

In those uncluttered days, the gentlemen of the Melbourne Hunt Club rode to hounds clear across to the suburb of Moonee Valley. After the chase, they gathered at the tavern, tethering their steeds to an old hitching rail, which stood on a patch of grass stretching to Collins Street.

In recent years a door was cut through one of the inside walls to make the serving of food easier. Workmen discovered that the walls were constructed of bluestone blocks two feet thick; four men were required to lift one. It would seem the old pub has every chance of outlasting its smart new neighbours.

But another old pub which may not be so fortunate is Mac's in Franklin Street. Built in 1846, it's astonishing, in fact, that it has survived so long with its wide verandah and general rural air. But Mac's is on land purchased by Trans-Australia Airlines—it squats in the shadow of their administration skyscraper. And there seems little doubt that one day the value of the site will mean the end of the old place.

Silverton

Horrible Gillespie had it down pat. He'd walked there before, y'see, carrying a fire hydrant to beat off the flies. "Got a ciggy paper an' a thumbnail dipped in tar, eh? Well, jot this down. Foller the dingo fence for a coupla hundred miles south and you're guaranteed to build up a bloody great thirst even if you haven't been eatin' the sand. Where the fence ends, you branch off south-east and you'll be crawlin' by now, but when you see a house cut fair in half—and, Jeez, did a champeen gargler live there!—you'll know you're set for a few coldies. Jist fall down the hill from the house and you'll roll into the public bar." Hmm. Well, lesser men than Horrible Gillespie can find the Silverton Hotel by driving twenty-one miles west from Broken Hill. It's the last pub west for many miles, and the bones of the gallant chaps who said, "I'm gonna have a couple down the road," still litter the sandhills. Or so the locals say, and would they lie?

Silverton is a romantic skeleton itself. The wind whispers in the ruins of stone buildings, and the rusted hulks of T-model Fords and suchlike, whose owners are no longer even a memory. But the pub, drawing parched throats from Broken Hill in their scores on Sundays, survives in great glory. The publican, George Weir, has a special Sunday licence enjoyed by several pubs beyond the ten-mile line from Broken Hill. And it is not surprising that the population of Silverton often increases fifteenfold on Sundays.

Facing page: George Weir, mine host at the Silverton Hotel

Once some 7,000 people lived there. They came to mine silver in 1882, and for a time it was a fabulous place. Seven splendid hotels lined the streets, but then they were destroyed by the Curse of Charlie Rasp's Sore Toe. For it was Charles Rasp who stubbed his toe on a rock a few miles away and unearthed a veritable mountain of minerals. The place came to be known as Broken Hill, infinitely richer than Silverton. So the people of Silverton gradually abandoned their town and migrated to the new bonanza across the flinty desert to the east. And one of those people was the gentleman who owned that strange half-house, and we can't name him for he may be still alive and 100 years old and waiting for some rotter to libel him.

The story is that he frequented the hotel and was often seen to squeeze the life out of a keg of beer. He was married to a shrew—all big drinkers are—who poured his dinner into his bed when he didn't come home on time. And such things. So one day, after she'd broken a few of his bones, he roared: "I'm shootin' through for good an' I'm taking along my share of everythin'." With mathematical precision, he chopped the stone house in half and departed with it (in numbered pieces, no doubt) on a bullock train. And her half of the house remains, a monument to the moral: if you're going to get drunk, don't go home until she's asleep.

The present pub, built in the mid-1880s, was once the post office. It has a smallish bar dominated by a massive bone inscribed, "Don't bite me, bite this," and a beer garden whose popularity depends on the intensity of the day's duststorm.

Indeed, they have experienced some fearful duststorms out there. "There was one, I recall," George said, "when four detectives came out in a car from Broken Hill. One of 'em had to walk beside thc car, because they couldn't see the white posts. That was a hell of a duststorm. You couldn't use the same glasses twice. By the time you'd finished your beer, your glass'd be full of dust."

It was so bad that several weaker souls did vacate the beer garden, and one chap was lost, never to be seen again, on his way to the Gents. This caused much annoyance, because it was his shout. And orderly shouting is a matter of great importance in the Silverton Hotel, as is illustrated by the story of German Charlie. He died, and his mates, wiping away a tear, sprinted to the pub with his estate gripped tightly in their hands. The four of them stood at the bar and, when every fifth round came up, the money would be ceremoniously extracted from German Charlie's pile. He never liked to be left out of a shout.

The Black Lion

Anticipating that some tourists would be far too faint-hearted actually to enter a real mine in Broken Hill, one man decided he would cater to their tastes. So he created a mine in a bar. It is a most genteel establishment (compared with the usual watering hole in the Broken Hill area). The gourmet can always dash away from his glass for a moment to savour such delicacies as "Oysters—Angels on Horseback." Not that we approve, of course, of mixing food with drinks. The pub is the Black Lion, just off the city's main street.

Licensee Bert Smith explained how it came about: "This used to be an old-fashioned men's accommodation hotel. Where the main bar is now was the dining room, a rough old joint."

Using sheets of aluminium foil, they lined the bar and produced an effect which is fearfully like the interior of a mine. There are even eight-foot rock bolts embedded in the roof and timber actually taken from the old North Mine. The

Yardman at the Palace Hotel

Black Lion's yardman, Bob Kendell, who spent forty-three years in the mines, said: "It's exactly like a real mine." It's a tribute to the authenticity of the place that he spends as little time as possible in there. And the city's genuine miners are conspicuously absent.

To round off the effect, there's a tailor's dummy, dressed as a miner and seemingly engaged in drilling at the wall. They have a confession to make about that dummy: it's a woman. "The only miner in town with boobs," said Bert.

The traditionalist who objects to aluminium-foil mine shafts can always partake of his refreshments in the splendid Palace Hotel, a short stagger away. Eighty-eight years old, sixty-three rooms on three storeys, it displays fine staircases whose wood was carted from the coast. And a yardman whose brother is a knight and one of the barons of the mining business. Its present publican is a cool cat named Earl Quinn. It has a Bistro and attracts the young swingers of the city. But the Palace is steeped in local history.

Many years ago four men died when a mine shaft at the back of the hotel collapsed. The escaping gas forced them to clear the bar. How many pubs can claim something like that?

Lou Richards

Everyone in town knows little Lulu. It's impossible to avoid him, leering out of your morning newspaper, making outrageous statements about football teams, and clowning it up on telly. That's our Lulu.

Lou's pub is the narrow Phoenix (once it had the charming name, the Fail Me Not Inn), in Flinders Street, close by the newspaper offices to which he contributes his wit. It's a newspaper pub: printers downstairs, journalists upstairs.

Just about everyone in town knows Lulu's family—Edna, his wife, Molly, his mother-in-law, and daughters, Kim and Nicole. And there's Val, who likes a beer before she cooks lunch, and Dorrie, who loves Peter McKenna, the champion footballer. Lou decks all the girls out in long dresses in Collingwood football club colours, black and white—you see, everyone in town knows that Lou was captain of Collingwood in the early 1950s.

Lou's a warm-hearted chap (though there are some who say he wouldn't shout if a shark bit him). But the author wouldn't say that. You see, Lou cashes his cheques.

THE AGE
DRY

The pub the ants built

Termites built the old Halls Creek pub. As the little creatures laboured back in the 1880s to construct their giant ant-hills—often taller than a man—they didn't know, of course, they would be helping to build a hotel.

But soon afterwards a man named Hall discovered gold near the creek, and the miners swarmed to the barren hillside. And, in the correct order of things, a pub followed them. Now, out in the desert, there was a great shortage of building materials until someone had a bright idea. So they chopped up the ant-hills into bricks—(having persuaded the residents to depart) and carted them to a site just above the creek. And there they built the pub and added a few mud bricks for variety. Soon every building in the settlement was constructed by the ants, apart from the tin store.

Nothing remains of the pub now, but the ant-made post office next door, doorless and roofless, still stands; it testifies to the ants' skills. The ants, in fact, have reclaimed the few remaining bricks at the hotel, swarming into the tiny caverns their ancestors built. Mrs Beryl McGuire was the last licensee of the old pub. She abandoned it in 1958 when the town was moved to a new site eight miles away.

"It was the first pub on the Western Australian goldfields," she said. "My husband and I went to old Halls Creek in 1952, bought the post office for £350, and lived there. Later we acquired the hotel. Oh, it was a fine old place! The inner walls were lined with galvanised iron, and we even had a ballroom. There were terribly smart race balls, and women in beautiful gowns would come from stations for hundreds of miles around. The ladies' lavatory was way out the back, and they had to find their way across rocks and sand to it. It was a wonder some of them didn't disappear into the desert. I remember the day my husband built a path to the lavatory before one ball, and the women were so overjoyed they clustered around to kiss him!"

When Mrs McGuire and her late husband (she has since remarried) abandoned the old place, they took whatever they could with them to their new hotel in the new town. The tremendous annual downpours eventually washed the old walls away. Part of the old iron roofing has been preserved in the new pub. Mrs McGuire gave up the new hotel some time ago and now lives in a house not far away.

"I do pine for the old place," she said. "I'd happily go back to it."

The Windsor

There was never any doubt that the Windsor in Melbourne would become a grand hotel. In fact, when the shipping magnate, George Nipper, began to build the hotel in 1883, he named it the Grand. The original architect, Charles Webb, also designed the Royal Arcade, Bourke Street; Melbourne Grammar School; Wesley College; Christ Church, South Yarra; South Melbourne Town Hall; and the Alfred Hospital. But, almost in its infancy, the hotel suffered an indignity that still outrages honest drinking men everywhere.

A temperance group purchased the hotel, and at the inaugural meeting, James Munro, who later became Premier of Victoria, dramatically held the liquor licence aloft and burnt it amid cheers and the clinking of lemonade glasses.

The hotel's historian notes: "Not until the Grand Hotel had been entirely renovated, renamed the Windsor, and again made the possessor of a licence, did it recover from the effects of this quaint demonstration." In his zeal to purify the pub, Munro (bless his non-alcoholic heart) did not take into account the habits of other Melburnians and, as a temperance hotel, the fortunes of the Grand Hotel slumped severely. Aflame, however, with their mission to turn it into a palace of wowserism, the temperance people almost doubled the building

a year after they had purchased it. By 1888 it ran along Spring Street, from Little Collins Street, almost to the White Hart Inn, at the corner of Bourke Street. And hereby lies the clue to the pub's future.

Sir John Monash, the great soldier, headed a company which bought the Grand Hotel after the first World War, and in 1922–23 the hotel merged with the White Hart and was renamed the Windsor. Operating under the White Hart's licence, the hotel entered its greatest years, showing the benefit of the $100,000 Sir John Monash's company had sunk into it.

The Windsor's close proximity to Parliament House has made it synonymous with the great political events in Australia. When Federal Parliament met in Melbourne, it is said several amendments to the Constitution were drafted in rooms in the Windsor. Politicians are still a familiar sight in the lounges—Sir Robert Menzies would stay nowhere else during his years as Prime Minister; and English cricket teams used it for many years. And there is a charming tale involving the hotel and Sir Robert Helpmann, the South Australian-born ballet dancer.

Helpmann came from an old-established pastoral family who would not be seen dead in any hotel other than the Windsor. As a boy, young Bobby spent many nights there. Many years later, having won world acclaim as a dancer, Helpmann went back to the hotel.

An old retainer met him in the lobby.

"Ah, Master Robert," he said, "and are you still in the cattle business?"

The hotel is still in excellent condition, and many of the original fittings remain. A feature of the dining room are the cupola lights, each ten feet nine inches in diameter, complete with cathedral glass, and costing only fifty-four pounds each when the hotel was built. A tribute is paid to the White Hart Inn which died so that the Windsor could rise again to glory on the fumes of alcohol, in the name "White Hart Grill."

The Old White Hart was built in the 1840s, and Samuel Halfpenny obtained the licence in 1847. It was characteristic of Melbourne hotels of the period—a simple, solid two-storey building with no room higher than nine feet from floor to ceiling. As hard as it is to believe today, the hotel was then on the outskirts of the town, and mine host of the period had to use all his wiles to attract customers to the bar. In 1850 Henry Lineham, who was then licensee, advertised a programme in which a goat race, a pig race, and a game of football found place. Activities, it will be noted, designed to make the throat dry from cheering or the body hot and bothered and in need of cooling.

In May that year, Henry Lineham advertised:

The Old White Hart Inn
Great Bourke St

This well-known OLD ESTABLISHED HOUSE *having undergone thorough repair and more extended accommodation for Visitors is now open and conducted by*

HENRY LINEHAM

who flatters himself that his reduced scale of charges to

NEWLY-ARRIVED IMMIGRANTS

is such as to give entire satisfaction to those who may take up their abode at the above Inn.

GENTLEMEN

from the bush and others, visiting Melbourne for a short period or otherwise, will find this one of the most comfortable, quiet and economical Inns in the city of Melbourne. The bedrooms and sitting rooms are conveniently situated to each other, affording the advantage of a

PRIVATE RESIDENCE

in a public Inn. The Wines, Spirits, Bottled Ales etc are inferior to none. The stabling is excellent. In short, there is first rate accommodation at the above Inn for both man and beast.

Today the same applies, although the horse could present something of a problem. But not one, mind you, that the staff of the Windsor would find insurmountable. A Melbourne journalist described them well in an article in 1971: "A black-uniformed luggage 'boy' who could be a year or two over pension age, moves at a stately pace to the reception desk, followed by a Western District matron giving queenly nods to Windsor staff retainers who may remember the day her father married her mother." Indeed, the Windsor made its name as a squatters' hotel. People like the Fabulous Falkiners, the world's greatest merino sheep breeders until they sold their holdings in southern New South Wales, were frequently seen there.

In recent years the Windsor has been somewhat overshadowed by the ritzier Southern Cross, a city block away in Exhibition Street. Most of the international notables seem to prefer the Southern Cross, and much of the corporate entertaining is carried out there. But there is more of a threat to the Windsor than simple competition—there is a danger that, one day, the hotel will be demolished. In 1971 an undisclosed buyer bought a 12·8 per cent shareholding in the hotel for $800,000, and it was feared that this may have been the preliminary to a takeover of the hotel. The hotel site is the big attraction; it has been conservatively estimated that the site alone would be worth $4 million.

A takeover would be a great pity, indeed.

Barmaids

Way up in the north-west, there's no more delectable a sight than the barmaid's bloomers. A man strides into a bar—he's a veritable walking duststorm—and the pastel panorama of a pair of panties signals a warm welcome, like a neon light outside a roadside cafe at night. He knows that relief is at hand—but don't leap to any wicked conclusions. That relief will be restricted purely to beer, or rum, or whatever refreshment has obsessed his brain over the past few throat-parching miles. Anywhere north of Meekatharra is Barmaid Country, and rarely will you find a man pulling beer.

And it seems the barmaids have adopted a flash of floral frillies as their stock-in-trade. A proud professional symbol—the badge that informs the thirsty traveller

Esplanade Hotel, Port Hedland

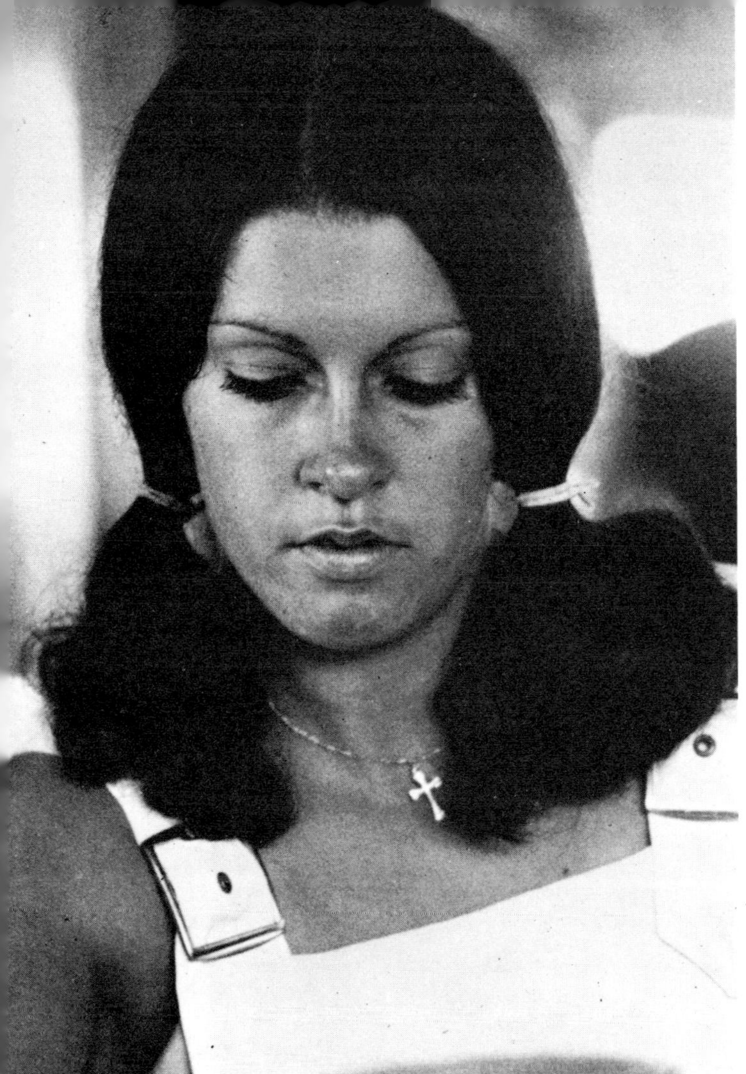

that they are, indeed, the true Queens of the North. Their skirts have remained remarkably short, perhaps a concession to the heat. They have scorned such fashion aberrations as midis and minis, and even hot pants. The best way for students of such important matters to observe the phenomenon is to take a position at the corner of the bar for an unrestricted view of the activities behind the counter.

Women students are permitted to take part in this research but are advised against making remarks, unless, of course, they are anxious to learn new, frank phrases from the barmaids' petal-like lips. Now, the idea is to wait until the barmaid is required to reach to a higher shelf for a bottle of rum. Up rises that ever-so-brief skirt, and Aaaah! The word passes quickly through the ranks of the patrons: "Paisley blue."

Another girl bends down for a dozen cold bottles. "Orange—must've just

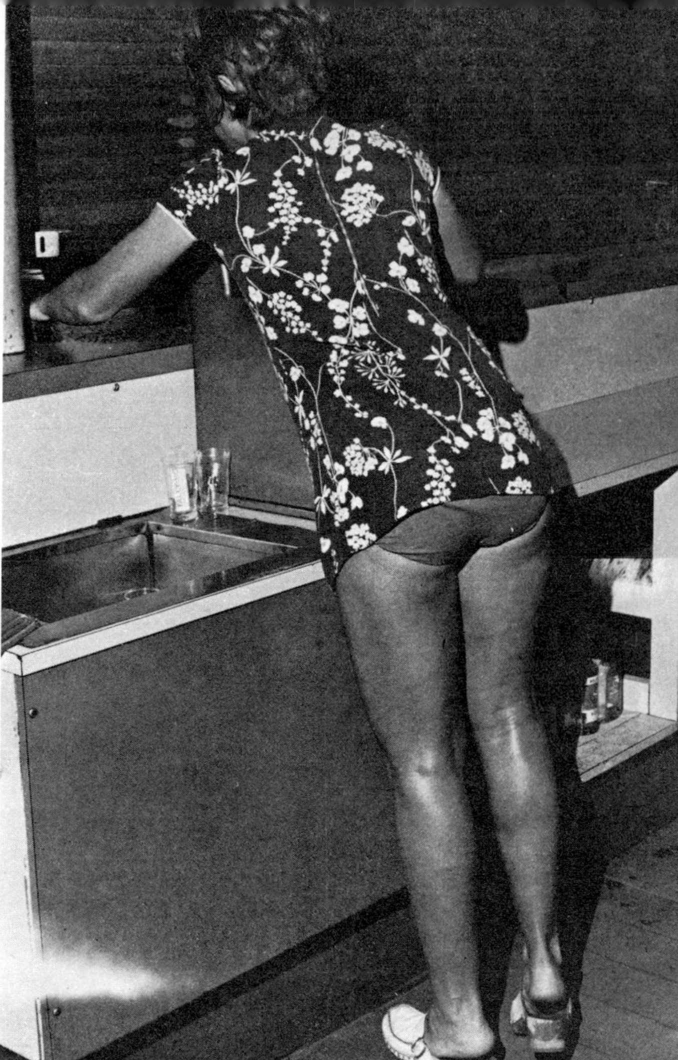

bought 'em. Haven't seen that pair before." If all this sounds a trifle perverted, that is exactly how it is meant to be presented.

The barmaids of the north-west are a mixed bag: a married girl from Perth who has come to the outback to be near her miner boyfriend; a university professor's daughter saving to go to England. They are an anonymous, itinerant race, known only as Faye, and Dawn, and Pat, staying a few months then moving on, always moving on. Packing their panties and disappearing in search of goodness knows what. Very rarely will you find a local girl working in the pub in her home-town.

But why the preference among publicans for girls? Stuart Dyke, licensee of the Esplanade Hotel, Port Hedland, had a quick answer: "Drinkers prefer to look at a pretty face, and girls are more reliable than men. They work harder and are less prone to get at the grog."

And why do the girls want to come to such inhospitable places to work among some very rough customers? Equally simple: eighty dollars a week less eleven dollars for full board. The girls are good at their job, and well they know it; they consider themselves the front-line troops of the pub game, ever so superior to waitresses and receptionists. Stuart Dyke employs fifteen, average age twenty-four. He said: "They demand rooms as good as the guests and they get them."

Most publicans, such as Trevor Bidewell at Fitzroy Crossing, hire their barmaids through agencies in Perth. If the girls stay for six months, in many cases they are given their return fare. They are all things; soft, imperious, detached.

Scene: The Continental, Broome.

Patron: "Give us a smile, love."

Barmaid: "I'm paid to pour beer, not smile, so shoot through."

Never, never patronise them. They hold your drinking future in their fast-moving hands; you need them more than they need you.

Bless 'em all.

Your father's moustache

Nutty Cook on drums, rat-a-tat! Carl Goff, banjo, ping-a-ding! And Bert ("late of Ted 'Eath's Band") Penn on the ivories! And away we go! Hic, burp, hooray.

Here's the place where troubles fade away,
Fun and games and music all the way,
Once you're here, you'll always want to stay,
So come to Your Father's Moustache!

Boomp, boomp. Fill up them jugs.

The East Perth Hotel on a cool Friday night, and the oldies are at it again: a couple of bowling clubs, George and Josie and the rest from down their street, a cast of thousands, in fact. Or so it seems. And the astonishing sight of middle-aged men actually enjoying a night out with the missus. Laughing together!

"Shut up!" Colin Fitzgerald, master of ceremonies, has taken the floor. Everyone is quiet, for he is Jim Gerald's nephew and if you don't know who Jim was you shouldn't be here.

"Right!" he cries, "Now it's time to trip the light fantastic. Select your partners for a foxtrot."

A young girl, who must have wandered into the room in error, says: "The foxtrot! Good God, what's that?"

Not so long ago the East Perth was an exceedingly unsavoury pub. Ladies could be found close by and they would agree, if asked nicely, to fornicate for small change in the bushes across the road. Fisticuffs were common, and State Government cocktail parties were rare. But one day the East Perth came into the hands of two very imaginative partners, Frank Baden-Powell and Coralie Condon. They are old-time theatrical folk, and their growing empire includes

Rita Hammond

such places as Diamond Lil's in Perth and Dirty Dick's in Sydney. Well, the East Perth wasn't exactly their glass of champagne, but they saw its potential. So they set aside a large room and opened Your Father's Moustache.

Oh, young people do go there, but it is essentially for their mums and dads. It drips nostalgia. A patron summed it up: "A few jugs of beer, a good feed, a good singalong, a few jokes about tits and bums." Parmelia, Chevron, and Wentworth should take note of that—the East Perth is always packed. Away with the expensive imported stars—bring on the tits and bums.

And there's also Rita. She's the wife of the East Perth's licensee, Bill Hammond. She's youngish, buxom, with a voice that sets the male patrons' bald heads aglow with hardly-remembered passions. She was six months pregnant on that cool Friday night—and that added largely to her charms—and when she unleashed "Frankie and Johnny" there was a cry of "Hubba, hubba!"

Then she was fluttering among the guests, gesticulating with her foot-long cigarette-holder, and making certain everyone was happy. Her wide, scarlet mouth bore a broad grin. She had come from Glasgow to East Perth to bring good cheer, and they all loved her for it.

For those who consider themselves a trifle too sophisticated for Your Father's Moustache, the Baden-Powell organisation has another little treat: the Pink Pig. It is a wine shop in suburban Subiaco, a haunt for the swish young groovers. No music, mind, but a great range of wines and an array of pork dishes which can be consumed in secluded little corners or the garden outside. An ideal place, said a man at the bar, to take someone else's wife—which he was doing.

The Pink Pig is not a pub, but its distinction is that it was Perth's first licensed wine shop when it opened in 1968. And it does have another distinction: a stained glass window from Frank Baden-Powell's old school, Christian Brothers' College in St George's Terrace.

The convict lady

Grace Curtain is the great-granddaughter of a devilish rum thief named Adam Sproul. And she is terribly proud of her ancestor.

After all, if it were not for the light-fingered Adam, Mrs Curtain would not even be permitted to be a member of an odd little group called the Broad Arrow Society, let alone its guiding light.

Grace's local is the Bush Inn at New Norfolk. Now, there is some confusion about the Bush Inn. Everyone knows a gentleman named David Bush started it in 1815. But the argument is: was it named after Bush or its rural surroundings? All that aside, it took a woman, Ann Bridger, to actually open the Bush Inn for business in 1825. She sounds a formidable woman, a widow who came to Van Diemen's Land with her daughter, also Ann, and apparently owned a fair sum of money. She also had a son, Henry, who had some connection with the police stationed along the Derwent River to watch for escaping convicts. Men like the bushranger, Martin Cash, hid in the hills near New Norfolk, and there is little doubt he would have partaken of the odd furtive ale in the Bush Inn before his face became too well known for safety.

Grace Curtain is perhaps the most formidable woman in New Norfolk since Ann Bridger. She lives in a convict-built stone house a short walk up the hill from the pub. Her house was erected only ten years after Ann threw open the Bush Inn's doors for business.

Many a person searching for Grace has sidled into the Bush Inn and, finding she is not there, has sought directions from a barman to her house.

For these are people with nagging doubts about their ancestry.

Any Australian who believes he is not, well, descended from the purest of free settlers, is well advised to consult Grace. You see, Grace's Broad Arrow Society—its membership was about 100 at the end of 1972—is restricted to people who can prove they have an ancestor transported to Australia, and to Tasmania, in particular, for such crimes as thievery, murder, awkward politics, or anything else which might have offended the stern British prosecutors.

"Oh, so many Tasmanians are terribly sensitive about their convict ancestry," Grace says. "I'm snubbed in the street by some of them and called a bloody idiot by others. The snobs don't like me rattling their family skeletons. But I'm very discreet. I never, never expose anyone's ancestry unless he gives me permission. But it's ridiculous that only 100 people have joined the society and owned up to their past when 67,000 convicts were transported to Tasmania alone. Any Tasmanian can find a convict in his past if he cares to look. My own ancestor, Adam Sproul, was a soldier in the N.S.W. Corps. He was noticed siphoning rum from a large keg belonging to the government to a smaller one of his own and was sent to Tasmania in chains in 1832. I'm terribly proud of him!

"Of course, some people are terribly keen to join. I wrote in our newsletter recently: 'Regrets to the many people still trying to claim a convict ancestor—keep trying—not much chance of missing out! And likewise to those who haven't the courage of their ancestors' convictions. Put yourself in his place—what would you have done? Well, we who are so proud of what our pioneers achieved find this hard to comprehend. One lady wrote saying her great-grandfather was renowned for soundly thrashing his wife and consistently bashing the kids—is this enough to gain her admission to the society? His crime was *not* being caught.' "

So if you believe you have a convict ancestor (and a good sense of humour), visit the Bush Inn and ask for Grace.

She'll take you home, peruse her files for your family name. And what she tells you about great-great-grandpa may send you fleeing back to the public bar for a stiff drink!

The Nullarbor Nymph

It is with some pride that we present for the very first time photographs which conclusively prove that the Nullarbor Nymph was not a figment of someone's imagination. She is pictured striding briskly through the famous white sand dunes south of Eucla, close to the border between Western Australia and South Australia, where she made her first dramatic appearance early in 1972.

She does look a trifle well-fed, doesn't she? Well, that can probably be attributed to the exceptional rains which promoted considerable green feed in the outback that summer.

There are some doubtful souls who may say that she looks suspiciously like a certain barmaid from the Amber Hotel at Eucla. But to those we simply say: "Shame on you." We were most fortunate to be guided to the Nymph's habitat by Ron Sells, noted bushman, who was among the first to sight her originally and who, by a slip of the tongue (accidental, most certainly) in the bar at the hotel, brought the attention of the news media of the western world to Eucla.

Some may recall his succinct comment when a gentleman from the British Broadcasting Corporation telephoned him in the bar one night and asked: "What will you do if you catch her?"

To which he replied: "What would you do if you caught a half-naked sheila running around in the scrub, eh mate?"

The B.B.C. man was lost for a reply.

It all began in the bar (where most true stories begin) when someone said

casually: "Did ya see that sheila in the nuddy 'cept for a kangaroo skin mini-skirt feedin' the kangaroos out there?"

"G'wan."

"Yep, beautiful she was, a luscious blonde."

Now, just by chance, a hot publicity man from Perth happened to be partaking of liquid refreshment at a corner table and, just by chance, he overheard this interchange.

And just by chance, the proprietor of the Amber Hotel, Lithuanian-born Steve Patupis, had a telex machine in his office. So the publicity man sought his permission to use the machine and very soon the sensational tale of the Nullarbor Nymph was landing in newspaper offices throughout the land. It wasn't long before newspaper reporters and television crews had invaded Eucla in search of clues, and Ron was on hand to render all the assistance he could.

And finally, they made *Time* magazine.

It transpired that many other people in Eucla had seen the Nymph, particularly after closing time. A man in Adelaide thought she might be his daughter, as she was very fond of animals and got on particularly well with kangaroos.

Eventually the excitement died down, and all the media gentlemen from the city departed without seeing her. They muttered words such as "bulldust" which did not refer to the surface of the road from Eucla to Ceduna. Ron went back to fishing for sharks, but he can still be found almost any evening in the pub ready to assure the visitor: "Oh, she's out there alright, mate."

Eucla and the Amber Hotel were most assuredly on the map. But even without the Nymph, the pub is a splendid one, and its future is assured. It stands on a hill overlooking the great Australian Bight and the sand dunes which are slowly devouring the old Telegraph station. From the hotel's first-class rooms at certain times of the day, the dunes take on the appearance of low clouds. The future of Eucla lies not in nymph-hunters, but in other big game men: the shark hunters. The world's biggest White Pointer shark ever caught on a line was snared at Ceduna down the coast, and the people at the Amber Hotel say their sharks are bigger. The hotel has accommodation of a standard high enough to impress any millionaire wanting to stay in Eucla while he pursues the big man-eaters.

The future of all the pubs across the once-notorious Nullarbor Plain looks rosy.

Many intrepid drinkers are scared off the plain because of the 300-odd-miles of unsealed road from Ceduna to the Western Australian border near Eucla. But the South Australian Government is expected to have the road sealed by 1976, and the Nullarbor Plain publicans are anticipating a bonanza. Steve Patupis is confident the traffic, now 7,000 people a month, will double when the road is bitumen all the way from Adelaide to Perth. And they'll most certainly be thirsty by the time they reach Eucla. A big new hotel is planned for Cocklebiddy, and the next oasis, Balladonia, will be rebuilt for the influx. After that, the drinkers will find solace in Norseman and the other towns of the goldfields which have been catering for giant thirsts for years.

So, good drinking. But watch out for the Nymph.

Facing page: Balladonia, Western Australia

The horse-breakers

John Achilles would rather have been in Brisbane, but he'd gone badly at the rodeos lately and was stuck for cash. So he was consoling himself in the bar of the Club Hotel at Chinchilla, Queensland.

"I drew a few crook horses," he said, "but my mates did all right. All us horsebreakers drink here, but I'm on my Pat Malone now. The others have shot off to the Big Smoke. Ah, we had a good time on the circuit, though. We got stuck in a boozer in South Australia, and at nine o'clock the old sheila who ran it took the till off to bed and let us cowboys take over. What a night!"

He sucked at his beer and gazed through the window at the railway yards.

"Not to worry, mate," he said, "My time will come again."

Berri's Community Hotel

It is Easter Sunday evening around seven o'clock, and the faithful are forming a ragged queue across the beer garden lawn, clutching their heated plates, and remarking on the tantalising aroma of chops and sausages sizzling on the griller under the canopy of the Grizzly Barbecue.

It's a very special night. Ernie's come up from Adelaide. For a mere $2.50, they're getting a plate of meat, a smorgasbord of salads, *and* Ernie. The queue moves oh, so slowly, but there are no complaints. And neither would the hungry stranger dare complain.

Because nearly every one of these patient customers is a partner in the hotel. It is their very own, and their pride is something to behold. They know that the profits from their $2.50 will be ploughed back into their town—for improvements to the swimming pool and the new caravan park. Also much of the money will go towards keeping the river bank beautiful so that Old Man Murray, whose water keeps their town alive, will have a pleasant place to traverse when he reaches Berri.

The punt at Berri. The hotel is on the far bank

With food on their plates, they are crowding into the dining room where the resident band, Strawberry Fair, is belting out the latest hits, and copious amounts of beer are being drunk. Wine, the local product—they have the biggest winery and distillery in the Southern Hemisphere—is conspicuously absent.

"Ernie, Ernie! Bring on Ernie."

A roll of drums and a hoarse cry from the announcer: "Ladies and gentlemen, Ernie Sigley, the greatest TV star in Australia!"

There he is at last, resplendent in a red sports coat. Everyone's delirious. Ernie sings a song, and says: "When I was driving up here I saw a lot of workmen and a truck marked 'Maintenance Patrol' and I thought, gosh, I can never get away." Everyone chuckles. They all know about Ernie's divorce.

The stranger is somewhat bemused. A girl near him leans across and whispers: "It cost us $250 to bring Ernie here. Just for the night—cop that!" She's a typist at a garage and a member of the hotel. "It cost me only fifty cents, and I get to attend all the openings here, like when we opened the new motel units, and I can go to the annual general meeting and make a fuss. Only I wouldn't, of course." Her girlfriend's in a daze. "She comes to all the big nights in Berri," says the informative typist.

Hush. Ernie's whipped in another one. "You know, when I got back from London last year, my wife had taken all the furniture," he says. "Well, I'm in love again, but I'm going to have concrete furniture next time."

Next morning there are very many hangovers. Malcolm Hill, the manager—he played for Sturt, the Adelaide football team—is presiding over the great clean-up.

"We have 330 members," he said. "They have to live in the Berri area and be on the electoral roll. We're making a drive for more members, in fact, because of competition from clubs. This used to be a privately-owned hotel, but in 1937 five local men raised loans from the banks and the brewery and bought it. The loans have been well and truly paid off. All profits go to improving the hotel or helping the town. From memory, $80,000 has gone back into the town in the past ten years. The hotel also pays for the upkeep of the river foreshore, and that costs us around $5,000 a year."

Berri, of course, is not the only town to have a community hotel in the Murray Valley, but it certainly has one of the finest. The community hotel employs seventy permanent and casual staff, a fair slice of the town's population of 5,000. Much of the profits come from the Adelaide well-to-do, who drag their boats to Berri every long weekend behind Jaguars and Mercedes. Buxom city girls, with their long hair trailing, slash backwards and forwards on the river behind powerful craft, but they have occasionally to stop to make way for the punts, which carry cars across from the south.

In the car park, Ernie's preparing to drive back to Adelaide and his television show.

In the foyer, they're tearing down the posters announcing his appearance.

A new face is being pasted on the board: Johnny O'Keefe. As the typist says with such feeling: "All the big stars come to my hotel."

Coca-Cola

Ceduna Community Hotel

Ceduna is another South Australian town with a highly-successful community hotel—and the local people made it their own even without the aid of outside loans. The hotel was originally opened in 1902, and several leading citizens received word that it was about to go on the market in 1949.

Led by Peter Morrison, chairman of the Shire Council, they called a public meeting and proposed that the people buy it.

Frank Tonkin, one of the group who wanted the hotel, said: "The whole town turned up. There was considerable opposition, particularly from non-drinkers, but eventually we won them over. We elected a committee of seven men to handle the purchase, and Morrison and I went to Adelaide to see the hotel brokers. We settled on a price of £23,000 for the hotel and £10,000 for the fittings. We didn't use bank money or outside loans; we simply raised the cash in debentures from people living in the shire. The debentures were in multiples of fifty dollars, and in nineteen years, we'd paid everyone out. It's done wonders for the district. We've just handed out $40,000 to the district hospital for improvements. The marvellous thing is that drinkers who mightn't normally donate to charity are doing it unconsciously. Oh, we had problems at first. They thought they owned the pub themselves and demanded free drinks, but finally they understood how it worked."

Chloe

Miss Cook's School for Young Ladies has a different role nowadays. It is the home of Chloe, dear Chloe, soft and naked, withholding nothing and temptingly virginal.

Chloe is the most famous pub nude in Australia, perhaps the most famous pub nude in the world. Chloe's regular lovers visit her daily and gaze at her over their beers; some can come only rarely—the middle-aged Americans who fell for her during the second World War hurry from Tullamarine Airport to visit her, to make sure she is still alright.

Chloe lives in Young and Jackson's Hotel at the intersection of Flinders and Swanston streets, opposite Flinders Street Station in Melbourne. Most of Chloe's lovers can visit her only briefly each day—the quick beer before they catch the train.

She was painted by Jules Lefebvre in Paris in 1875, won the Grand Medal of Honour at the Paris Salon, and was sent to Melbourne for the Great Exhibition in 1880. Chloe herself, in the meantime, is said to have taken her own life. Mr (later Sir) Thomas Fitzgerald, a surgeon at the Melbourne Hospital, bought Chloe. Norman Young purchased her for 800 guineas ($1,680) in 1908 when Fitzgerald died.

Norman Young and Henry Jackson, who made a killing in New Zealand mining ventures, were art lovers who filled the hotel with every conceivable type of painting. The pub sits on the busiest corner in Victoria on a plot of land which was a Crown grant to John Batman, founder of Melbourne, in 1838, and for which he paid the princely sum of £100.

The present building is thought to have been erected about 1840 and was a hay-and-corn store, butcher's shop, and Miss Cook's School for Young Ladies. In 1861 John P. Toohey opened its doors as the Princes Bridge Hotel. Today almost lost under its burden of neon signs, Young and Jackson's is synonymous with Melbourne—and Chloe.

ELECTRICITY
makes life easier!
MUTUAL
Bradmill
sheets
PETER STUYVESANT
SWANSTON ST

Captain Moonlight's local

There are three gravestones on the hillside at Overland Corner near the ochre pits where the Aborigines painted their faces and bodies, and one stone has been preserved more lovingly than the others. The inscription reads:

Walter Brand,
Youngest and beloved son,
W. and M. Brand,
Died, November 24th, 1880,
Aged four years.
A bud to bloom in Heaven.

Little Walter Brand choked on a potato in the kitchen of his father's sandstone tavern at the foot of the flinty hill where his grave lies. His resting place overlooks the Murray and the awful, inhospitable plains beyond. The Brands built their pub in 1859, and the formidable country is testimony to their courage. Until it lost its licence in 1897, its tiny bar rang to the cries of the riverboat men and their rugged drinking companions, the overlanders driving cattle from New South

SACRED
WILLIAMSON WRIGHT

Above: A cool glass at Doyle's Beer Garden, Watsons Bay, New South Wales

Right: Young and Jackson's, Melbourne

Facing page: The Nullarbor Nymph, Eucla, Western Australia

Above left: Ron Sells, alleged to
be among the first to sight the Nymph

Above right: Steve Patupis,
proprietor of the Amber Hotel, Eucla

Above: Cooling off at Crossways Hotel, Katherine, Northern Territory

Left: Swinging night, Stuart Arms Hotel, Alice Springs

Facing page: Publican's wife, Marble Bar, Western Australia

Above: Kiandra, New South Wales

Left: Variation on a theme, Fancy Dress Ball, Tennant Creek, Northern Territory

Facing page: Downing a can, Fanny Bay, Darwin, Northern Territory

Left and below: The cricket match outside the pub at Mataranka, Northern Territory

Wales to the Gulf. And if little Walter Brand had lived, what tales he would have told his grandchildren.

The face of a bearded man with mad eyes stares from a poster behind the bar. Below the face are the words:

Andrew George Scott, alias 'Preacher Scott', alias
CAPTAIN MOONLIGHT
— Outlawed —
Whereas ANDREW GEORGE SCOTT, *alias* CAPTAIN MOONLIGHT *(also known as 'Preacher Scott') did unlawfully seize control of the Overland Corner Police Station and subject Mounted Troopers to imprisonment therein . . .*

The Overland Corner was Captain Moonlight's local pub. The acknowledged expert on the bushranger is Mrs Eleanor Cole, who now cares for the pub for the National Trust of South Australia. "Oh, he'd ride his horse in here quite often and cause disturbances," she said, "and he would never dismount. The story was he'd leave the back and front doors wide open so that if the troopers came in, he could ride straight out and make his escape through the mines on the hill." And what of little Walter? Did he crouch behind the bar and quake in fear when this terrible man crashed his fist down on the counter? Walter would have been three when Moonlight seized the police station.

It is a pity that special licensing arrangements cannot be made for the Overland Corner. Such is its appeal that when a special open day was held in September 1971, 2,000 people turned up to revel in its history.

The beer farm

Beer, beer, and beer is what the Matthew Flinders is all about. Rivers of it. Flowing from a score of kegs, squirting from forty nozzles, and down fifteen hundred gasping throats.

"Right-oh, whose shout?"

The Matthew Flinders, which rose in functional splendour in the Melbourne suburb of Chadstone in the late 1960s, is the greatest beer farm in the land. Oh, it does have some pretensions to gentility. There's a replica of Matthew Flinders' log in the lobby and a cannon from *La Estrabella,* sunk off the Santa Cruz islands in 1788.

But the statistics are the thing at the Matthew Flinders. In the gigantic public bar alone, they fit at least 1,000 people on a good night—supervised by eight black-clad karate experts. And that's not all. There could be another 500 or so in the other bars and dining room where the food's fine and the house champagne costs four dollars a bottle.

The beer leaves the cellar through a bracket of tubes, cooled to near freezing by water-encircled pipes. The pub has seven miles of beer piping to get the amber fluid to its forty outlets.

In a hot week the patrons can be relied upon to empty 250 eighteen-gallon kegs and 3,000 dozen bottles from the drive-in bottle department. It is a record no other pub in Victoria can match.

And few pubs pay a licence fee like the Matthew Flinders. It is related to the amount of beer sold, and the pub's annual bill ranges from $54,000 to $57,000. Need we say more?

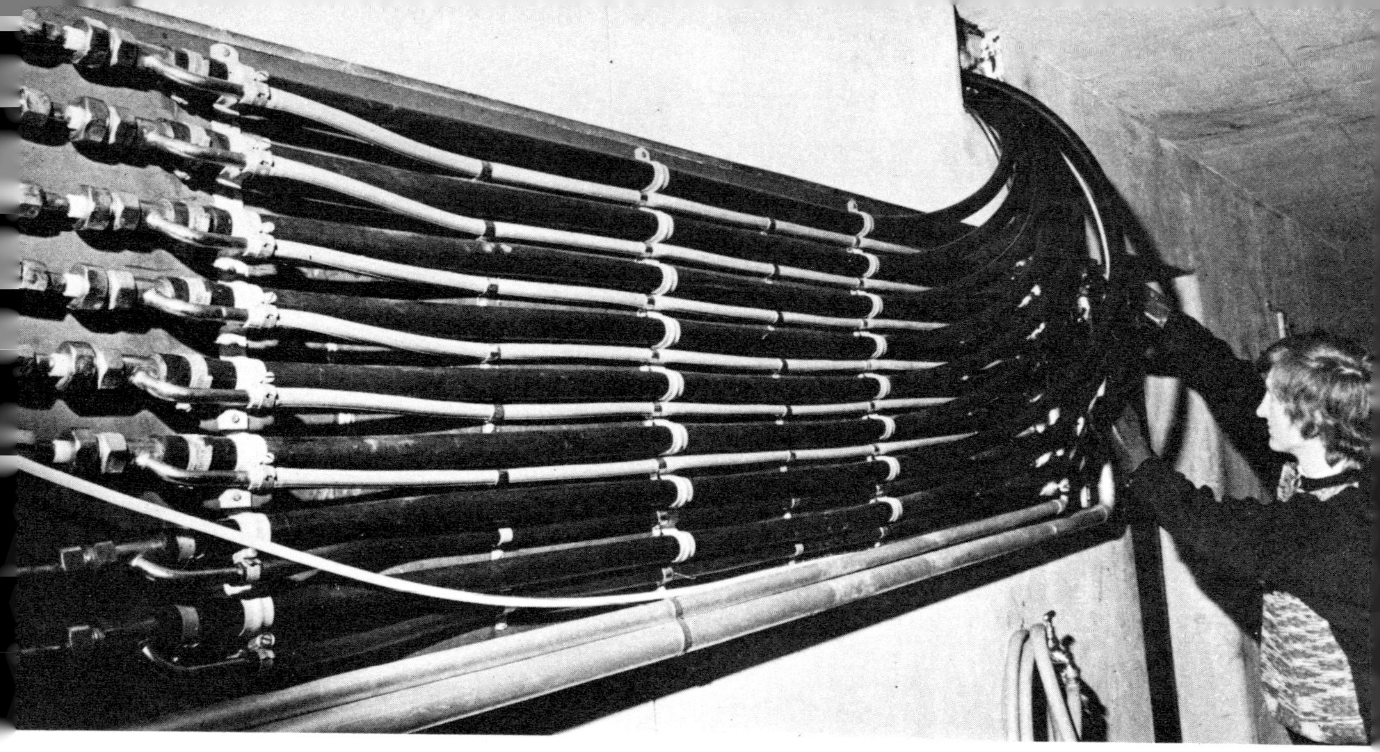

Customers in the Matthew Flinders

The cricket match

There was a bit of a row at first when the lads from Katherine (who caused a mild sensation themselves, mind you, by arriving in whites and real cricket caps) insisted that the Mataranka boys would ruin the pitch if they wore riding boots. After all, the Katherine team had carted the matting sixty miles in the back of a utility. But for the sake of peace, they allowed riding boots, because that was all the home team had.

The match began after a beery lunch. They decided to hold it in the road-train park outside the Mataranka pub because, as the cook from Mataranka homestead,

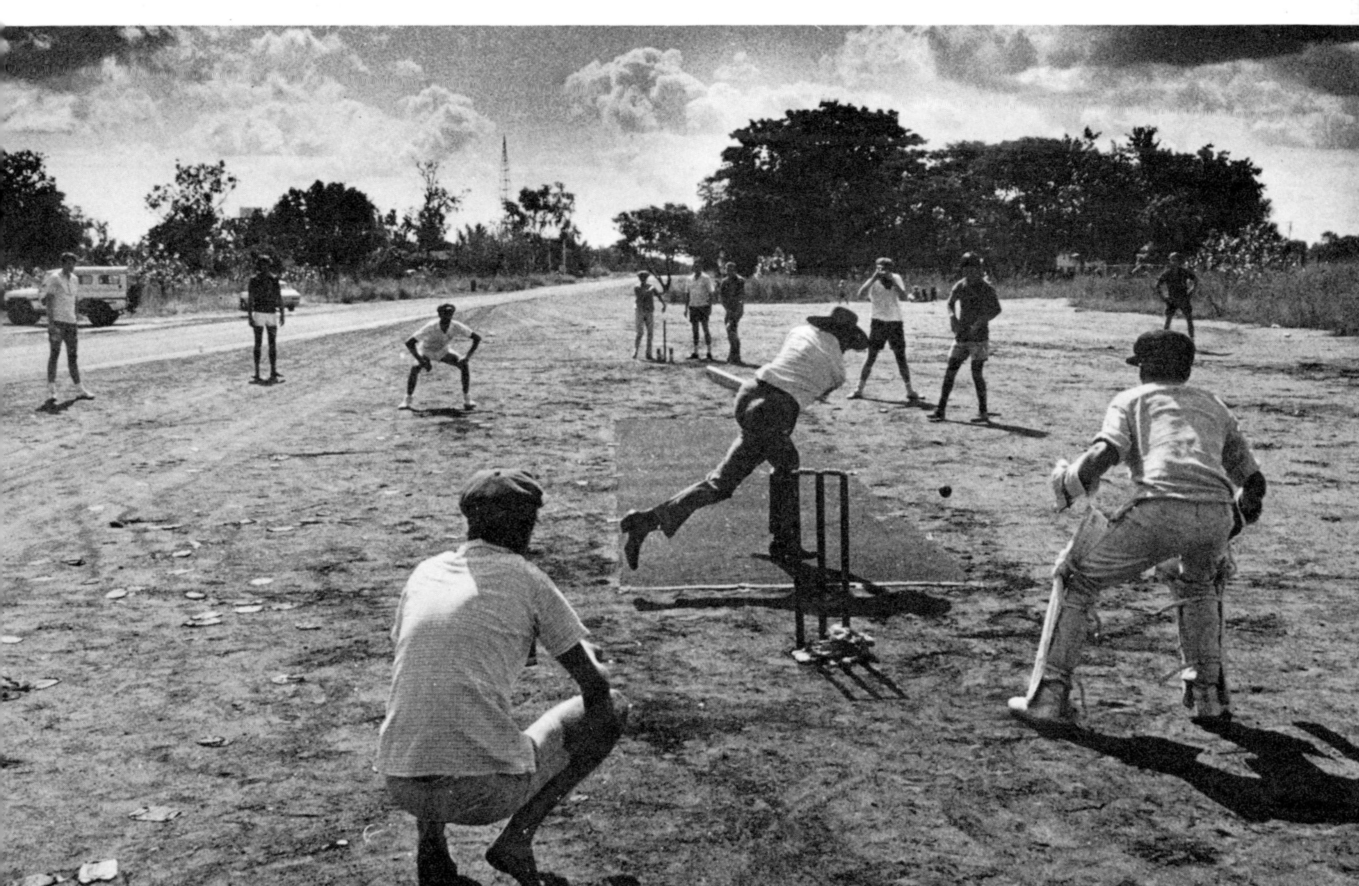

Dinah Vallier, explained: "They wouldn't have been able to get hold of the batsmen quick enough, if they held it at the racccourse."

They had only four stumps so they stacked up two pillars of beer cans at the bowlers' end to make up the numbers. And then they stationed the cover fieldsmen on the Stuart Highway with a short fine leg carefully placed to direct traffic.

The rules (and they'd neglected to consult Don Bradman) were simple enough: a six if you broke a window at the pub or hit a road train (and if you broke a road-train windscreen, you had to fight the driver, too, during the tea break).

Furthermore all fieldsmen had to carry a can of beer in one hand to even things up, because the batting wasn't too hot and every batsman had to make at least one run before he was out. Which all seemed fair enough.

Oh, and one more clause: after every six, the batsman had to bolt down a can of beer. This, the umpire explained, was to ensure that no one wielded the willow too proficiently.

"Y'see," he said, "they've all got a fair skinful already and they'll be nice and rotten after they've skolled a few. Even Garry Sobers couldn't make more than twenty here, mate."

McKenzie, the publican, opened for the locals. The first ball, which was thrown but no one cared, stayed low so he decided to fend it off with his pads.

Except he wasn't wearing any.

They adjourned while temporary repairs were effected to his battered legs, and someone yelled: "Do ya want a bloody splint?"

Few wickets were falling, but that could be explained by the fact that the bowler had to shout for anyone he dismissed. As the afternoon progressed, one chap tried to sneak back to Katherine, but the slips formed a cordon in front of his car and pushed it back into the car park.

"You can't leave until you've had a bowl, mate," they said. After all, it was 33°C under the Moreton Bay fig where the spectators sat, and the bowlers were expiring rapidly.

At last, the final batsman was out—the manager of Mataranka Station had legs so bowed after many years on a horse that one of the Katherine bowlers slipped a leg break through them. Then they all went to the pub to hoe into a bullock.

Footnote: One bloke did know the score, but he'd forgotten by next morning, wouldn't you know!

Hadley's

For thirty years, Hadley's Hotel was up for sale. But no one wanted the old place.

In the 1950s its then owner, Arthur Drysdale, even tried to get rid of it by putting it up as a prize in a raffle. But the winner scorned the great pub and instead took $400,000 in cash.

Hadley's is the sort of grand old place which could well have a heart. If so, that heart would have broken in those unwanted years.

But now Hadley's is coming to life again. Oh, certainly, its original clientele would throw up their hands in horror. But no matter; survival is more important. Federal Hotels have taken over Hadley's and, behind its austere walls, the youth of Hobart are cramming into new, swinging bars. The man behind all this is the manager, Ray Farmer, who came to Hadley's in his mid-twenties, introduced young, attractive staff, and brushed the cobwebs off his ancient charge.

Hadley's started out as the Bedford Arms Inn in the early 1850s under one John Webb, then official caterer to Government House. It was built on the site where the Royal Marines camped at the founding of Hobart in 1804.

Webb's fine reputation quickly drew the town's more fashionable citizens to the hotel. He had an ice house on Mount Wellington, from where he brought ice

daily by pack horse. Its social prominence was capped in 1861 when the Tasmania Club made the hotel its headquarters. And its standing received an even greater boost just five years later when the Duke de Penrieve, a member of the House of Orleans, and Australia's first Royal visitor, chose to stay there. In the 1870s there was a succession of proud advertisements—electric light in every room, then later, a telephone on every floor.

In 1881 J. C. Hadley bought the hotel, and it became Hadley's Orient Hotel. The family operated the hotel until 1919, and since then it has had several owners.

There must have been times when Hadley's came very close to demolition. But it hung on tenaciously.

Long live the oldest of the grand hotels in the land!

Tilpa, New South Wales

The priest came down from Bourke in the afternoon, and the faithful hastened to polish off their stubbies and follow him into the parlour of the Tilpa Hotel. Their faces were angelic, and few lips bore traces of beery foam. In the bar a few yards away, those who confined their worship to the breweries made a conscious effort not to blaspheme, for the next hour at least.

It was a regular Sunday evening in the Tilpa pub, Back o' Bourke and southwest a bit—an island in a sea of dust and emus and flies. A stranger came in and nodded when the publican, Stan Garland, asked if he wanted to drink out of a glass. And the locals nudged each other and grinned, and tilted their twenty-six-ounce bottles to their lips.

A sign, BAA, painted on the window announced that this was, indeed, the bar; beyond it lay the flat where all fights were conducted and, thereafter, absolutely nothing for one hundred miles west to the old opal settlement of White Cliffs. And on the wall of the bar, a poem:

The wonderful love of a beautiful maid,
The love of a staunch, true man,
The love of a baby unafraid,
Have existed since life began.
But the greatest love,
The love of loves,
Even greater than that of a mother,
Is the passionate, tender, and infinite love,
Of one drunken bum for another.

Stan Garland said: "We always have church in the parlour, and the priests and brothers come from Bourke or Wilcannia. When it's over, the priests join the lads in the bar—for a glass of orange juice." And he winked.

Jack Robinson, Tilpa

We're waiting for Tilpa's living legend to make his appearance and finally we are rewarded. A tall, old man, the great Jack Robinson, who swam his horse three miles through the 1970 floods just to get his brawny hands on the last two stubbies in Tilpa. It appears he is shy.

"Nah, I'm not so tough. Why there was one bloke here, I remember. He was diggin' a well on the other side of the Darlin' when it collapsed and broke his leg. So he climbed out, hitched his horse to his dray and drove into the pub.

"It was in the mornin', and someone said: 'What are you doin' in here so early?'

" 'I broke me leg.'

" 'Oh.'

" 'I'll 'ave a whisky.'

"So he finished his whisky and goes over to see the Bush Nurse, but she wouldn't set it. It was a real bad break. When you'd hit his knee, the leg'd swing loose. The Bush Nurse reckoned it was too hard for her to fix, an' anyhow, he shouldn't have gone to the pub before goin' to see her. So he went out the back and got an old kerosene case. Remember them? Anyway, he broke it up and set the leg himself, and we all had a few beers, although we didn't make him shout that day.

"He was the toughest man I've ever seen."

Old Jack himself is regarded with some awe in an area where even the women lift bags of wheat. When the Darling burst its banks in 1970 and licked around the kitchen door of the pub, he was a few miles out of town at his shack and it occurred to him he'd like a beer. In fact, he'd love one. So he saddled his horse Kelly and sallied forth, licking his parched lips. They came to the flood water and for seven miles they walked through it until finally the game steed had to swim with Jack still astride him.

"Then suddenly he was fightin' for the bottom. He was sinkin' and blowin' bubbles out of his nostrils so then I reckoned it was time to hop off. I swam the last mile meself, and Kelly made it on his own. I got to the pub, and they'd all shot through so I drank the last two stubbies I could find. And me and Kelly swam home."

Largs Pier Hotel

Venus gazes vacantly from the wall and is temporarily distracted from the task the artist has given her of using her fleshy wiles to convince Adonis he should abandon his hunting trip after all. Perhaps she has taken a fancy to one of the smooth-jowled young Adelaide businessmen partaking of his luncheon below her.

Ah, no, she seems far too worldly. That young businessman would be far better suited to one of the coy virgins tripping side by side from the orphanage in J. Haynes-Williams 1879 work, "The Foundlings," on the other wall.

On any weekday, the business gentlemen of Adelaide can be found enjoying the fare in the luncheon room set aside for them at the Largs Pier Hotel. If it were not for their crisp suits of the 1970s, the scene could well be taking place

ninety years ago. Little else has changed. The Adelaide *Observer* of December 1882 reported the opening of the Largs Pier Hotel as follows:

"The bar is furnished most elaborately with silver plate backs, raised panelled cedar counters with heavy mouldings and trusses, pewter tops and brass facings."

Very nearly all present and correct in 1972, but where are those silver plate backs? Oh, well. . . .

"The bathrooms are fitted up luxuriously with hot, cold and salt-water. . . ."

Regretfully, the salt-water is no longer available (though it's only a short dash across the Esplanade to the beach).

". . . fire plugs on each floor and speaking tubes to the bar."

The speaking tubes have given way to the telephone, a ghastly invention.

"Facing the railway platform and flagstaff is the Largs Pier Hotel, a handsome structure, containing fifty rooms without offices. It is three stories high and has two lookout towers. The building is classical Italian style with boldly projecting cornices . . . handsome trusses . . . ."

Definitely all present and correct ninety years later. And for that we should be eternally grateful, because the Largs Pier is a truly magnificent hotel steeped in the city's history. Today it is leased from the South Australian Brewing Company by the Pierce and Matthews organisation, hoteliers extraordinaire, men with a love of the past and a flair for bringing it alive today. They lease or own eighteen hotels in South Australia, a little empire that had its foundation soon after the second World War.

The stage was set in 1939 when the youngish Seymour Matthews went to Whyalla to take over his first hotel, the Bayview. He struck up a friendship with another, older publican in the town, Tom Pierce, and in 1945 they joined forces, based largely on Tom's money and Seymour's imagination. Seymour has two sons, Guy and Tony, both in their thirties, both St Peter's Old Boys, and both imbued with their father's enthusiasm for the old and charming.

Guy, the younger brother, now has the Largs Pier (in the Pierce and Matthews tradition of each one running the pub he fancies). They took the hotel in 1954 and restored it from dilapidation to its present, near-original splendour.

"It was in shocking shape," Guy said. "The pigeons had been left unmolested on the roof for years, and we had to remove two tons of their manure, shovelling it straight over the side into trucks below. One of the previous publicans was a pistol fanatic and he liked to sit in his office and blaze away up the hall at cards stuck on the cedar-panelled wall in the bar. He was a good shot—he could knock the middle out of an ace of spades—but he'd made a mess of the panelling nevertheless. But we can be grateful to him for one thing. He occasionally

Feathers Hotel, Burnside, South Australia

liked to turn a spotlight on the roof and blast the pigeons. There might have been a lot more manure if he hadn't given them an occasional burst."

They bought "Venus and Adonis" from the Port Adelaide Art Gallery and installed it in the hotel in 1954. They secured "The Foundlings" in 1968; it had been passed in at an auction earlier for $1,500, but Seymour picked it up later for a mere $300. From the entrance hall, a passage leads to the main dining room. The passage is decorated with nineteenth-century collages by Theo Townsend, and they depict Queen Victoria and other ladies of the period in stately habit.

And in the dining room, there's a real surprise, something of a mystery, in fact. A painting of a woman by Jacques Vaillant, who was born in 1631 and is believed to have died in 1691. He worked in Rome, Vienna, and Berlin, and at one stage held an appointment under the Elector of Brandenburg. Seymour bought it in an Adelaide furniture store for $300 . . . but who is the woman? The dining room also has the hotel's original cedar sideboard, and several of the gilt mirrors are to be found hanging around most of their hotels; they are, in fact, the Pierce and Matthews symbol now.

The Largs Bay Company built the Largs Pier Hotel to accommodate newly-arrived settlers and people awaiting the arrival of ships. The company also constructed the pier, the Esplanade, and several shops. The hotel was incidental to their shipping interests, but someone in the company seems to have had sufficient influence to guarantee that no expense was spared.

The hotel, including stabling (still there in part), ostler's house, and coach-house, cost £11,000. To that, add £8,000 for furniture and fittings alone! The first landlord was Thomas Hixson and he must have considered himself a very fortunate man, because just three days after the hotel's opening, a regatta attended by some 8,000 people from Adelaide was held off the pier. The Adelaide *Observer* reported: "The Largs Pier Hotel must have made enough over the bar to pay for a long succession of off-days, judging by the crowd craving cool liquor." The grog had such an effect that people fought with each other for places on the return train to Adelaide that evening.

Guy Matthews, who has done considerable research into the hotel, believes it became something of a white elephant after its heady beginning—a great, ignored monolith by the seaside. Nevertheless, two years after the opening, it had lost none of its initial style, as a dinner menu of 1884 testifies:

Oysters [which would have been dredged from
Oyster Bay on the other side of Spencer Gulf].
Soup a la reine printanniere.
Flounder or Flathead.
Kromeskys of Veal, Truffled Partridges,
Cutlets a la Duchesse.
Boned Turkey with Celery Sauce, Saddle of
Mutton, Roast Duckling with Olive Sauce.
Asparagus, Wilding Duckling.
Swiss Pudding, Stanbury Souffle.
Cheese croquets, Stilton, Lemon Water, Ice.

Gentlewomen had come down to the Largs Pier Hotel to await the return of their husbands, who were in Europe on business. But ship arrival times were uncertain in those days; they might wait a week, or more. Every morning they would congregate on the lookout towers; rugged up against the chill wind off the bay, they would pass around a telescope. And as there was no sign of the vessel yet, they would go downstairs to a quiet, unhappy breakfast. One can imagine them, listlessly picking at the truffled partridges.

The Largs Pier does have a new section—a vast lounge bar beside the original building. But it detracts in no way from the old. Guy Matthews has maintained the Largs Pier's association with the sea in this bar with a series of sketches by the South Australian artist, Chris Hall, of disasters and other nautical happenings which occurred within sight of the hotel: the collision of the British barque *Dimsdale* in 1912 with the Wonga Shoal light, in which the two lightkeepers were drowned; the collision between the *Ardencraig* and *Norma* in 1907 when the *Norma* sank with a full load of wheat; and a sketch of the gloomy hulk *Fitzjames,* which was moored off the hotel until 1888 and had, at one time, served as a reformatory for boys.

Originally the hotel had little narrow cubicles for single men on the second floor, but now they have been converted into larger rooms by demolishing the walls between them. On the third floor, two-room suites with separate bathrooms, toilets, and showers have been created, and most have French windows to the wide balcony.

Guy Matthews' elder brother, Tony, has charge of the unique Feathers Hotel in the smart suburb of Burnside. It is unique in that it is a hotel which contrives not to look like a hotel—more like a bank. And that is the way the residents wanted it. Tony Matthews, who leases the hotel on the firm's behalf from the South Australian Brewing Company, said: "The brewery tried to get a hotel in Burnside for many years, but polls of the residents continually rejected it. However, they finally agreed, as long as the hotel had the facade from a city bank which was being demolished. This proved too expensive, of course, so the brewery decided to build a Georgian Hotel which looked like a bank." There are a couple of discreet signs indicating that it is a hotel. But they could easily be missed by the uninformed. Feathers opened in 1966 and is now liberally littered with Seymour Matthews' artifacts—mirrors, prints, and paintings.

Tony Matthews was also associated with the family's lease of the marvellous Northern Gateway Hotel in Port Augusta. It is a former brewery-turned-cordial works and has been renovated without any of the original atmosphere being lost. House guests step from their rooms in the courtyard on to a sturdy timber platform which was the brewery's original loading deck. From here, mule-drawn waggons took the kegs to pubs in the town and to pubs in the desert to the north.

Down the coast

Surfers Paradise, jug country. Glug-glug, and back in the bloody queue again.

The sun presses down on the bare backs in the beer garden.

"For Christ's sake!" says the heavy-breasted blonde, "if you weak bastards won't pour it, I will. We don't want the bloody stuff to boil."

It's fast work, drinking beer in jug country. The higher the sun rises, the faster they pour. Nothing worse than warm beer. ("Makes you chunder.") Nevertheless, the last glass from the jug always tastes like warm tea. The Gold Coast is vintage, vulgar Australian boozing territory. It is an overrated, tatty, glossy strip of sunshine. After a few days, boring, monotonous, and sordid if you want it that way.

The pub's the only saviour. And the big beer garden at the Surfers Paradise Hotel, in particular. Sit back and study the mob, pairs of girls, pairs of boys; pick-ups are always imminent, and the Country and Western group's not half bad.

QUEUE FOR JUGS HERE.

"Your turn, mate."

"Hell, not again."

If you want a girl, take a jug to her table. But watch out. Like as not, she'll put you under the table (and you won't be in any state to grope at her thighs).

Two big bikinied brunettes came in from the beach at eleven, a hamburger each at noon, and they were on their eighth jug by mid-afternoon. Their unsuccessful seducers had long since faded away, glassy-eyed. The girls left at four. ("Need a lie down. Full up to here. When I walk I feel like a bloody washing machine.") Their gaze was a trifle fixed, but they were steady on their feet. What boozers! You felt like clapping.

(Around the pool at the Chevron, across the way, the same ritual is being carried out in a more respectable manner. The well-to-do laze around the garden, cigars, swollen stomachs, oiled, flabby thighs. The occasional beauty. The waitress swishes past in a ground-length printed cotton and a dozen pairs of male eyes turn.)

Dusk at last. The best pub's at Southport. But, what the hell, let's stick to Surfers. Tonight might be the night for the grand adventure. Or maybe tomorrow night.

The youngsters stream into the Skyline Lounge at the Chevron where the big groups play. In the shadows, near the ticket box, a policeman waits, peering into faces and alert for the under twenty-one drinkers.

It's the hunting hour. At the Surfers Paradise Hotel, the mid-twenties and thirties gather, the single and not-so-single, but who gives a damn about that. Eyes meet, look away, the big come-on, the sharply whispered: "Go away, I'm waiting for someone else." Oh, she doesn't know that someone else's name yet (she probably never will). But she's hoping against hope for the handsome stranger, the James Bond, the one who will whisk her away for a night of bodily contact. And on the beach tomorrow, their eyes will meet in daylight, and they will both look away. It will be all forgotten.

On your way south a few days later, you come upon the Coolangatta Hotel, the only really charming one on this desperate strip of coastline. Facing one street is a narrow little country pub, barely wider than the car parked outside. The locals are here, overalls and the like, calm and chatting. Walk up a lane beside the little pub and you discover that the Coolangatta Hotel has a severe split personality. Suddenly the country pub bursts into a splendid resort hotel. But unspoiled, not the least bit vulgar. A good cut of a pub.

Bogga Young and the game of darts

Albert George Young, better known in the Territory as Bogga, seldom plays darts these days. After all, he did lose a pub on a bad throw once.

Bogga's getting on now, and often you'll find him sitting in the shade outside his pub at Pine Creek recalling that awful night.

"I had the Commercial in Katherine and one night in '48 I was playing darts with Bill Fraser, who had the other pub in town. The way I remember, we were playing for ten quid a throw, and I didn't have much dough so I was borrowing tenners from the till—until it ran out.

"Bill had this real good idea. He said, 'Since you haven't got any money, how about we throw for a year's lease on the Commercial.' Like a bloody fool, I did, and when we finally called it quits, he'd won six years off me. He took me pub, and for six years I went contractin' and in the end I walked back into me pub and said, 'Right, now I'm back in. The six years is up.' So I got me pub back."

Ten years ago Bogga sold the Commercial to Swan Breweries. And what a sight it was! Gaping holes in the fibro walls where angry men had tested the strength of their knuckles. Today the Commercial has disappeared completely. In its place the brewery built a superb hotel in the Dutch style, bars galore, and a quick dash from one of the stylish rooms leads directly into the pool.

Not the sort of pub you'd risk in a game of darts.

Bogga Young, Pine Creek, Northern Territory

Kiandra

Once upon a time Kiandra had a courthouse and lock-up. And nearly twenty years ago they converted that building into a pub.

Which, in the eyes of any drinking man, gave the place at least some measure of respectability. To remind us of the consequences of too much of the cool amber fluid, there are still traces of the court and cells today.

This quiet pub gazes across the wooden skeletons of the deceased village. Kiandra is feeling the bust following its second boom. Way back in 1859, 2,000 people came to this bare alpine mountainside to scratch out the alluvial gold; they took 172,000 ounces, and by 1861, only 250 people remained.

But nearly 100 years later new diggers came and gave the old town a kiss-of-life. The men from the Snowy Mountains Authority arrived and carved dams and tunnels out of the mountains. But the scheme is all but complete and the hard-drinking workers have gone.

The pub remains, but it is surrounded by death.

The Grand National

Paddington is a marvellous place to drink, eat, and frolic. Go to the Grand National, at the corner of Underwood and Elizabeth streets, for lunch in the backyard, where you sit around white metal tables with a panorama of chimney pots above. Cook yourself a steak over the barbecue and be a glutton with the salad. Then settle back and speculate on your neighbours—they're doing the same about you.

That couple there. She is older, isn't she? Whispers. "I wonder who's looking after her kids." "Oh, don't be so nasty, Jocelyn."

The barmaid wears hotpants and sips beer with her friends. It could be you. Paddington is a friendly place. Evening comes, and the gay crowds cannot accommodate themselves in the bars of Paddington so they spill cheerily on to the streets. Beer and claret, that's the score.

"Hey," someone says, "let's go to Kandy's!"

Yes, let's go over to Kandy's in Woollahra. . . .

Kenneth "Kandy" Johnson is a publican, but surely the most sensational and unlikely publican in the land. In a country where publicans are, by tradition, broad of back, strong of arm, and big of belly, Kandy is a delightful, shattering contrast.

Kandy greets his customers in drag; to the uninitiated, he could be the prettiest girl in any room. Dressed as a woman, he promenades about Sydney, and when the police come to visit his hotel, he'll greet them, as likely as not, in glorious, feminine Technicolour.

"I'll tell you my life story," says Kandy. "I went to an awful, erratic school called Canterbury High School where they took you in with a marvellous, jolly high I.Q. and sent you away without any I.Q. at all. Anyway, I became interested in personnel work, and when I was going to a school for personnel officers, I'd attend parties, and people would say, 'Go on, do something, Kandy,' and I'd put on a pretty dress and a wig and do a number. Oh, I got the name Kandy when I was in National Service—the others thought I was so sweet.

"Well, some friends of mine decided to open a place. Do you remember a place called the Jewel Box which Lee Gordon, who was a marvellous entrepreneur, was running? Well, he had acts with drag people, and I appeared there one night. But the Jewel Box was common with sailors and that sort of person. Anyway, in the meantime, these friends of mine had opened the Purple Onion in Kensington, and I started working there. I did three shows with them, though I was still going to technical school at the time. I was doing so well in the clubs I decided to give tech. school away and did a season at Les Girls, where I wasn't all that happy. So I opened my own place called Kandy's at Enmore. In those days, I was working strictly as a comedienne. I thought straight drag people were rather foolish. Oh, I wore long gowns. Joan Sutherland was just hitting the headlines then, and I did her thing in a white gown and long wig and sang operatic numbers with my finger stuck in a bottle. All that routine.

"Anyway, Kandy's sort of sent the Purple Onion broke, and they were going to close, but instead we did a deal, and I closed Kandy's and became a partner

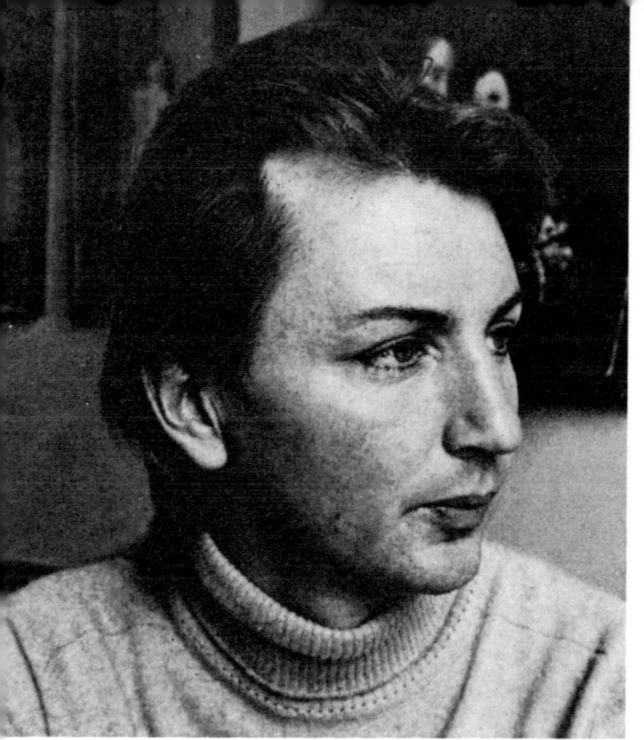

LEFT: "Kandy" Johnson. RIGHT: Kandy and the boys

at the Purple Onion instead. Anyhow, I didn't get on well with the boy who was the other partner in the Purple Onion at the time and eventually, I suppose through devious means, I became its sole proprietor and remained there for six years. It was a very good business, and we did very well out of that. But I got tired of it. We'd do a season with one show, and I'd think, 'Christ, I'm glad that's over,' and then we'd have to start another one. So I started thinking about running a wine bar but, when I looked at them, they were all so sordid and I went into hotels. Oh, I was terribly foolish then. I thought my grand reputation would carry me to success. I had great trouble getting a licence, anyone who'd been in night clubs and wanted to go into a pub was vaguely suspect—and they also suspected the Purple Onion of something they weren't quite sure about. The licensing police never got into the Purple Onion because we never had a liquor licence. People used to bring their own grog.

"They never quite knew what went on at the Purple Onion. All they saw was a thousand queens going *wheee* in through the doorway, and a thousand drunken queens coming *wheee* out the doorway! They never ventured in there. The place was efficiently run, and I never bothered them.

"But I got my licence and went into my first hotel, the Lord Roberts. I didn't think I'd have to perform any more, and it was there that I made a big mistake. I had the British concept of a publican-cum-artist. I thought I'd just have to stand behind the bar and people would say, 'Let's go and see Kandy, won't it be lovely.'

"I didn't realise that if I wanted to play Miss Aloof, I'd have to have the right sort of room around me. Las Vegas decor, that sort of thing. The Lord Roberts just wasn't me! So I chucked up a little stage and started to perform again, and people began coming to see me. Oh, it was a different sort of clientele from the Purple Onion. Lots of square people started coming, and I discovered they just wouldn't cop me funny. They just wanted to hear me speak.

"They wanted to come in with a mate and say, 'Eh, good sort isn't she?' and wait for me to speak. And when I spoke they'd dig their mate in the ribs and scream, 'Ha, ha, see, it's a man. And you said you wanted to root her!'

"I became the good-looking, fast-talking sort of number, a bit like Eve Arden. We'd get a hundred people in the room, and you couldn't get near the bar for a drink. The other publicans in the district *loved* me! Their clients would rush away, catch my show, rush back, and drink twenty beers, and then rush back and see me again. I was hardly selling a glass!

"Oh, getting back to when I applied for my licence—a lot of people said, 'Kandy, don't do it. They won't have you. After all, you're a female impersonator.' Oh, if I'd had one conviction, I wouldn't have had a chance. They even went back to my schooldays checking on me. They even dragged up a relationship I'd had with a young lady with whom I lived in a *de facto* situation for about nine months—it all came out in court. They said if I'd lied and said I was married, then I couldn't have been an honest person."

But Kandy won his licence and after his fairly unhappy experience at the Lord Roberts moved to Kandy's, at 88 Oxford Street, Woollahra.

"I wouldn't like you to say that all the patrons of Kandy's are lesbians and queens. It's more, well, a collaboration of all the oddest people. . . ." He waved his arm about the big lounge bar. "You might have two tables of lesbians over there, and a table of sailors there, and a table of queens there. And the straight people that can cope, they come, too.

"All these people get on very well. Oh, we do have our fights, but you have those in any pub. I trade on being a female impersonator who has a very well-run pub. When I go out, I dress as a woman. I feel more acceptable dressed as a woman. I have a better time. But I don't allow anyone to make the mistake of believing I'm really a chick. If I go out in drag, I like to go somewhere where I'm acceptable, but I can't think of anywhere in Sydney where someone might say, 'I'm sorry, Kandy, you can't come in dressed like that.' "

Perhaps there are those who feel they would like to go to Kandy's one night and make trouble, shout smart remarks. . . .

Kandy has thought about that, too. So he employs three very large gentlemen to watch for such people. And they don't wear frocks!

On the road to the Barossa

Jimmy You-Make-Ali, the Afghan hawker, Black Charlie, the swaggie, and all the others are but dim memories in the gentle valley now, but the dear little pubs they frequented still beckon. From Wilmington, east of Port Augusta, through Murraytown, Laura, and Clare to the vineyards of the Barossa Valley, it's a paradise for the traditional drinking man: the sort of chap who likes a quiet corner, a ticking grandfather clock, a publican with time to talk, a darts board rather than a pool table, and an English piece of country (even though the names may be German, or anything else).

CLARE + HOTEL
CLARE
HOTEL
beer
IS BEST

TANUNDA
HOTEL
HOTEL
AUSTIN
MORRIS

Perhaps the newest of the pubs in the district is Austin Condon's North Laura Hotel. It is thirty-seven years old, built in the solid traditional manner of locally-quarried rock. His family took over the original North Laura in 1928; it would have been 100 years old this year, if they had not pulled it down and built the new place next door.

Further south there's the Taminga Hotel at Clare, and not far down the main street, the Clare Hotel. Superb stone structures, enough to send a thrill of pleasure through the traditionalist. And finally, through the Barossa Valley to Balogh's Lyndoch Hotel, a precious, century-old stone gem set among the ripening wine grapes.

It is the place to spend a week or more, gossiping over a score of bars.

Black Charlie liked it so much he spent his life there. And the pubs were so dear to him that he carried a sugar bag containing fifteen pairs of boots so he would never break down in transit between pubs.

The Rose, Shamrock, and Thistle

Charles Burrell was deported from England to Tasmania for stealing a butcher's knife. He served his time, came to Melbourne, and took out the first licence for the Rose, Shamrock, and Thistle in 1854.

His early days as a publican were marred by tragedy. In June 1854, soon after he opened the hotel, the *Argus* reported:

"The friends of Mr Charles Burrell are respectfully invited to follow the remains of his late wife to the Melbourne General Cemetery. . . ." She was twenty-seven and left three small children. Between 1855 and 1927, eleven other people held the hotel. It was an important wayside pub, the first overnight stop for the Cobb & Co coaches on their way to Yea, and subsequently, Sydney.

Even when Patricia Negri's father, Ben, took over the Rose, Shamrock, and Thistle in 1927, it was still very much a country inn.

"There was just the pub and a shoeing forge next door," she recalls, "and every afternoon, an old woman came and milked the cows opposite. Outside the pub there was a horse trough where dad threw the recalcitrant customers. We had one customer, an English remittance man nicknamed the Mudlark, who lived in a humpy on the banks of Darebin Creek. He'd come in, stinking, order a beer and before he could drink it, dad would throw him in the trough. It was the only wash he got."

Patricia Negri married Craig Middleton, and they run the pub together now. They're both extremely proud of its past and have done wonders retaining its original appearance, particularly since the bush pub of Patricia's youth is now part of the suburb of East Preston, with housing developments stretching many miles beyond.

Patricia and Craig Middleton

Poppa of the far west

The story of Poppa Corones, a man who helped civilise Queensland's Far West, is the classic tale of the penniless immigrant who took himself in desperation into the wilderness and found his El Dorado. The day we were ushered into his presence, he had just turned ninety-two; he was deaf and near-blind and could not remember the date, or even the year he arrived in Australia. But there were many who knew his story probably better than he.

We left him alone with his thoughts and went to marvel at what he had achieved. To understand what Poppa Corones did, one has to understand Charleville. Even in the 1970s, Charleville is a dry, rough town, 1,000 miles inland over treacherous roads occupied at night by kangaroos and wild pigs that play havoc with a car if they chance to step in the way. Charleville is the last town of any real consequence for travellers swinging north-west to the rich mines of Mount Isa. And motorists are warned not to venture into the

badlands due east of the town unless they warn police of their planned movements. Such is Charleville in the 1970s.

Yet Poppa Corones went there and worked away diligently in the first decade of this century. Then he built a pub that set eyes a-poppin' from the Simpson Desert to the Pacific Ocean.

Nowadays Poppa's grand hotel is run by his son, Peter. It is almost unchanged from the day it was built in 1928–29, from the ballroom (once the finest outside Brisbane) to the suites with their ponderous furniture and plumbing which gurgles hollow abuse when disturbed in the night. The clientele has changed little in character, too; the sons and grandsons of the men who patronised Poppa's establishment when it first opened, and cattlemen in uniform, light-grey, felt hats with turned-down brims, check shirts, green trousers, and elastic-sided boots. Their Santa Gertrudis stock are selling well, they have money in their pockets, and they are spending it once again at Corones Hotel. And the pub is a happy place.

Peter said: "My father came from Greece at the turn of the century. He once told me he remembered leaving his ship in Sydney and walking up and down George Street and Pitt Street in search of accommodation. He couldn't speak English and he was having no success and finally he began to make his way back to Woolloomooloo. But he came upon a man cleaning the window of a shop that bore a Greek name. He spoke to the man in Greek and finished up cleaning the window and getting accommodation with the shopkeeper. He married a Greek girl in Sydney and went to Brisbane where he worked for a Greek who had a fisheries business. Then he went to Charleville."

Why Harry Corones (the Poppa came much later) would want to go to a place as desolate as Charleville is uncertain. Anyway, he opened a Greek cafe on Willis Street which happened to be opposite a rambling, one-storey structure, the Hotel Norman.

As he wiped the tables in his cafe, he would often stare through his window at the Norman and dream of building his own hotel there. He did so well at business that in 1912 Perkins Brewery offered him the lease of the Hotel Charleville. He kept the hotel for ten years and when he gave up the lease, he had £13,000 cash. So he bought the Hotel Norman and embarked on his grand project.

He tore the Norman down, and in 1929 a fine new hotel opened on the site. Corones Hotel had cost £50,000 to build—a vast sum in those days. He was immensely proud of his hotel and issued a booklet about it under the title: "Quality and Service."

Poppa and Mrs Corones

Peter Corones, Corones Hotel, Charleville

The booklet stated: "Hotel Corones, which has risen phoenix-like on the site of the old Norman Hotel, has a frontage of 210 feet on Willis Street, and embraces almost the whole space from Edward to Galatea streets, in Charleville. Five years ago, the foundations were laid, and today, this magnificent white building, costing in the vicinity of £50,000, stands—an outstanding feature in a progressive town—as the best-equipped and most up-to-date hotel outside the metropolis."

There was a barber shop, a rapid service of stock and commercial news from Brisbane, a foyer with copper-topped tables on a gleaming white marble floor, and a dining room for 150.

"The private bar is screened from the public section by an ingenious arrangement—the partition being in French polished oak with mirrors. The ceiling is in fibro-plaster, artistically designed; the beams in heavy Grecian Key, while the cornices are of Egyptian Cameos."

And there was the ballroom: "Attached to the hotel is a large dancing hall, with a floor unexcelled outside Brisbane . . . this spacious room is capable of seating 320 at dinner."

In 1932 G. B. S. Falkiner, of Haddon Rig Station, had such a pleasant day at the Charleville races that he hired the dining room and the ballroom and invited everyone he knew for dinner and a ball. It cost him around £500, a trifling sum for one of the Fabulous Falkiners, once the world's greatest merino sheep breeders. One ball nearly came to an abrupt end when a young chap who had over-imbibed rode his stock horse into the ballroom. The animal panicked and slithered across the highly-polished floor, tearing gorgeous gowns imported at great cost from Brisbane. It caused almost as great a sensation as the night during the second World War when an American Air Force officer, incensed at the din coming from a noisy gathering near his room, began discharging his revolver down the corridor. The bullet-chipped walls tell the tale.

Corones also played host to one of the great con-men who ventured into the outback—a man who claimed to be a Flying Doctor from Broken Hill. He established himself in the hotel with a flourish of pound notes and rapidly became a much-sought-after guest for social functions. Then he drew his trusty cheque book and took half the town. One of his better purchases with a dud cheque was a fine racehorse, surrendered to him in good faith by a local grazier. The Flying Doctor disappeared, never to be seen again.

The forty-room hotel had its lean times during the late 1960s and early 1970s with the rural recession, but when the cattlemen came good again so did the hotel.

"We're their club, their mecca," Peter Corones said. "We just can't do without each other."

Shaw Bay Hotel

Tom Fenwick, by all accounts, was a vain, imperious, demanding man. As harbourmaster at Ballina towards the end of the last century, he was a man accustomed to having his own will prevail.

In 1892 he had a fine house built near the water's edge at Shaw Bay, for himself, his second wife, and eight children. A fine house, indeed. In fact, the finest house on the northern New South Wales coast. It was constructed from the best local cedar; the marble in the entrance hall was imported from Italy. And Fenwick effortlessly paid a bill of £7,000 for the work.

Fenwick is said to have made his fortune by demanding outrageous fees from ships' captains to supply tugs to bring their vessels safely into port. "If they refused to pay," says Mrs Ann Weir, present occupant of his house, "he simply left them to founder."

Eventually even Fenwick had to meet the call of his Maker, and his house became a boarding school for boys in 1918. Later it became a boarding house. But the house deserved a better fate than that, and in 1950 it was turned into a pub, and what *more* important role could it fill?

TOOTHS BEER

Mrs Weir presides over the remnants of Fenwick's mansion. Admittedly, the enthusiastic renovators have taken their toll over the years, and the old sea dog would barely be able to recognise its exterior. But inside, much of its original extravagance remains—the double cedar stairway, the splendid fireplaces, and odd pieces of furniture.

A juke box rests on the marble and under the very eyes of Fenwick and his wife, so to speak. The harbourmaster indulged his vanity by having their portraits installed in stained glass in a window high above what is now the bar area. Fenwick chose to have himself portrayed as a feminine, delicate soul—and, as Mrs Weir says: "It's difficult to tell who's the wife."

One feels rather glad that the vain old bully finally had his picture hanging above a pub. Undoubtedly, it would give him the horrors if he knew.

Cedar stairway, Shaw Bay Hotel

The publican under siege

We should have minded our own business. It was mid-afternoon on the Brisbane waterfront, and we were backing, shoulder to shoulder across the back bar of the pub, in the hope that we would eventually reach the doorway and safety. Time passed so slowly. An Aboriginal girl was screaming at us, but we could not understand her words, and a huge Torres Straits Islander towered over us and clenched and unclenched his right fist.

We did not know how drunk he was (if he was in fact drunk at all), but his speech was even and clear.

"You take a picture, and I'm gonna break your face."

Okay, okay. You win. No pictures.

"We're all on a bond. You take a picture, and we go back to Bogga Road."

We were nearly at the door. The cameras were hanging innocently at Bruce Howard's waist.

"You did take a picture!"

The fist was brought back. The arm quivered. Then it was lowered, and he faded into the crowd.

The publican, William Hughes, was standing beside us now. He waved one arm placatingly at the crowd. The other held a firm grip on his monstrous German Shepherd: to all appearances a languorous dog named Bobo but with eyes which darted hither and thither.

We went to Hughes' private bar where the whites stood on carpet and drank in peace.

I said: "Did you take a picture?"

Bruce said: "Yes."

The publican shook his head in disbelief.

"Mad," he said.

The Hotel Adelaide on the river in Brisbane, was the toughest pub we visited in 25,000 miles. Oh, there are surely tougher and rougher pubs in Australia, like those along the Barbary Coast in Cairns. But we visited those before the patrons came growling in and filled up with fighting fluid. A man's not entirely stupid, you know.

William Hughes is a very brave man. His family's upstairs quarters are sealed off with a Cyclone fence topped with barbed wire. A publican under constant siege, he moves nervously.

"Many fights in those other bars?"

A wry smile. "Yeah."

"Do you ever go in without that dog?"

"I try not to, but sometimes you don't have time to think."

"Much of a fighter yourself?"

"I try to make 'em think I am. I've never heard of the Marquis of Queens-

Bobo and Bill Hughes, Hotel Adelaide, Brisbane

berry." A friend chips in: "He's the dirtiest fighter in Brisbane—every time he fights, he shits himself."

The Hotel Adelaide is what Australia is all about, whether we like it or not. A hang-out for Aboriginal outcasts, petty thieves, prostitutes, and violent people. Like flypaper, the back bar draws the worst whites who come to prey on the Aborigines, to steal their girls, and to start fights.

Hughes said: "This pub goes back a long way. Around thirty years ago it was called the Royal Mail, but a lot of ships from the Adelaide Steamship Company

Jennifer and Esther, customers at the Hotel Adelaide

stopped at the wharves over there and the pub got a lot of custom from them. So they changed the name. The coloured thing goes back to the war, I think. All the darkies were restricted to this side of the river, and the American negro soldiers came here. They taught our darkies. This mob aren't representative of Australian Aborigines—heck, they could just as well be a lot of bad whites. It just so happens the blacks all drink here. They're drop-outs, bludgers, will-nots: will not work, will not conform.

"I don't like it here, but I'm hoping that one day this licence will be moved to the suburbs, somewhere more palatable. I live upstairs with my wife, a teenage daughter, and three boys. The customers don't get up there. That's mainly why I've got the dog. My daughter goes to one of the best schools and every night she comes back to this. I've tried to help the darkies, but it's so discouraging. You can't treat 'em like ordinary white people; they confuse kindness with weakness. They're so accustomed to being punched and kicked down that they can't handle ordinary friendliness."

We got two of the Aboriginal women aside, and they talked for a pot of beer each; they were suspicious and they did not hide their dislike of us.

"What's your name?"

"Jennifer."

"Jennifer who?" Silence.

"Okay, just Jennifer."

"Yeah, she's Esther."

"Why do you come here?"

"All my friends do."

"Is the publican fair to you?"

"Yeah."

"Is this the only pub where the publican's fair?"

"I dunno."

"Do you feel safe in this pub?"

"Yeah, it's safer here than in the posh white pubs."

"What do you do for a living?"

"We're both on widow's pensions."

"What do you talk about here?"

"Our kids and our troubles."

"Do the police come here much?"

"Yeah, every night."

"Do they give you any trouble?"

"I dunno."

The pub and the fence

This is the sad tale of the pub and the fence. It seems that there is a pub, the International by name, in the South Australian city of Port Pirie. This tavern is directly opposite the wharves where men load ships with ore and, as the day progresses, become increasingly thirsty. So in the past many of these men would dash across to the International to quench their thirst, and the tills rang gaily to the tune of their coins.

Until one day a man built a fence, a high security fence to stop unauthorised people going on the wharves. So the gentlemen from the wharves could no longer take a short cut straight to the pub, but instead had to use a gate half a mile away. Which happened to be near another pub.

And the International lost half its customers just like that.

Sometimes the manager, Brian Boundy, is heard to remark: "I'd like to put in a gate and give all those wharfies a key." But it hasn't happened yet.

Facing page: Brian and Sandra Boundy, International Hotel

Hoppy Tom

Hoppy Tom had to drink alone. Oh, his mate had been with him earlier, but suddenly the door of the Warialda pub (New South Wales) burst open, and in stormed his chum's wife.

A giant of a woman; six axehandles across the backside, and biceps like a buffalo. She grabbed her elfish little spouse and lifted him right off the floor, his little legs flapping.

"You're coming home, you louse!" she roared.

But he was a man of spirit. He raised a fist, shook it, and cried: "Put me down, ya bastard, or I'll job ya."

Sneering, she carried him away.

However, out the back where they were playing cards, there occurred an event to cheer any male chauvinist pig. At precisely 8 p.m., a woman stormed in carrying a plate of meat and vegetables and slapped it down in front of one of the players.

Tearfully, she cried: "If you won't come home for dinner, you awful man, I might as well bring it to you here!"

A deathly silence.

Slowly he turned, looked at her and said:

"Where's the bloody gravy?"

Facing page: Top: Hoppy Tom. Below: Hoppy Tom (right) and drinking mate

The Tantanoola Tiger

In the tiny hamlet of Tantanoola, in the south-east corner of South Australia, there's a pub called the Tiger. And on the outside wall of the pub, there's a sign: "Tiger on display inside." Which takes us back to the end of the last century.

For some months in 1895 sheep had been disappearing without trace around Mount Salt Station, near Tantanoola. Nothing was left but a pool of blood. Then someone saw a massive dog tearing at a sheep's carcase. Quickly word passed around, and a great fear swept the farmland.

It was said to be like a tiger—cruel fangs and a powerful body. Children were escorted to and from school, and women drove their buggies to the stores in Tantanoola and Millicent with shotguns on their laps.

A bushman named Tom Donovan and three friends—it was said they could all extinguish a candle at 200 paces—set out after the tiger. They trailed the beast for weeks until on 21 August 1895 Donovan caught sight of it. Bending low he followed it through the scrub until he was within range. Then he killed the beast with a single shot through the heart. The "tiger" was brought to Tantanoola and put on display at the hotel, then named the Railway. People paid sixpence a time to gaze with awe at its striped coat and ferocious teeth.

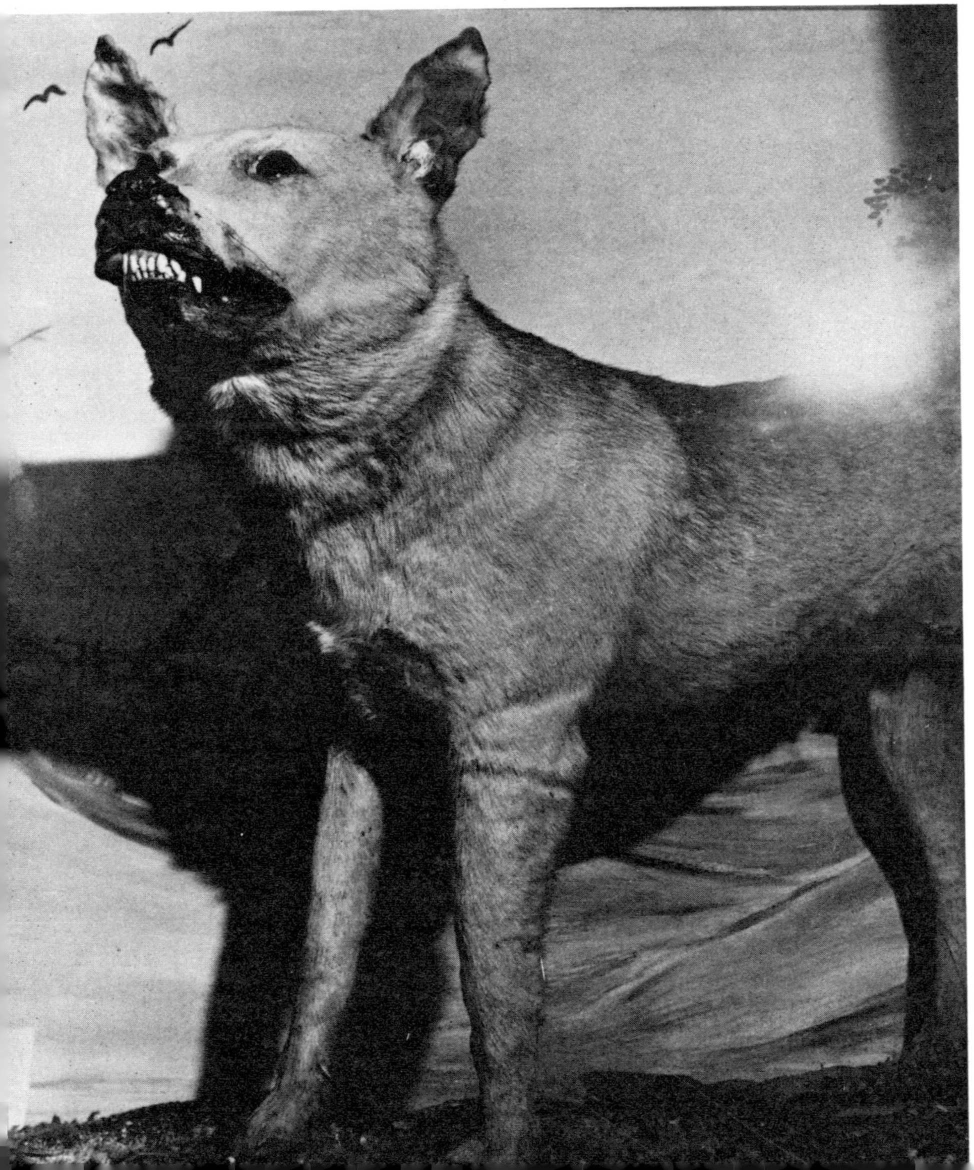

Bob Hart, present licensee of the pub, said: "It is widely believed now that the animal was an Assyrian wolf and probably escaped from one of the many ships which were wrecked along this part of the coast." The tiger, five feet one inch long and thirty-two inches high, was stuffed and displayed at the pub. It is today exhibited along with Tom Donovan's Winchester rifle.

There is also a visitors' book in which people pen such witticisms about the tiger as "Looks like my dad," "Looks like my old girl," "No comment," and "Bloody awful."

Such was the interest in the tiger that the name of the hotel was changed to the Tiger in 1905. Bob has carried the theme further by wallpapering the entire bar in yellow and black paper and making the wolf look deceptively like a real tiger.

However, the story of the tiger did not end with its killing in 1895—and has not ended yet.

In 1911 the rotting carcases of several sheep were found at Dismal Swamp, near Tantanoola, and the panic revived. Was another tiger loose in the bush? Not so. After some time a man was charged with stealing seventy-six sheep; he used the ruse that another tiger was on the prowl. He was sent to prison.

And little was heard of the tiger until August 1971 when Mrs Ruby Lepley and another elderly woman from Kalangadoo said they saw *two* tigers near Tantanoola.

Spend an evening in the pub staring at the wallpaper, and it is guaranteed you will see hundreds!

The pistol club

The rain came down in buckets, and every track out of Winton was impassable. So the road-train drivers went to the Central Hotel for a drink. Three days they were stuck there, that handful of gallant men.

And when they left, the publican, Geoff (Mr Wonderful) Thompson, gathered up all the rip tops from the cans they'd emptied: sixteen hundred of them.

And they made a chain forty yards long and hung it around the wall of the bar. Then they sent for some more cans—just in case it rained again. Meanwhile the locals settled down to add to the chain. They are a fine band of drinkers—Peeper Shaw, Guts Shaw, Castlemaine Perkins, Irene, Horrible Gillespie, Horsehead Clarke, and Jacyn Strictpussy (can that really be her name?), the barmaid who keeps the supplies flowing.

Every so often, one of them disappeared through a door marked "Pistol Club" (Drink till Midnight, Pistol Dawn).

ABOVE: Raffle prizes, Central Hotel, Winton

BELOW: The Pistol Club, Central Hotel

Kalgoorlie

Jim Larcombe rested his elbows on the bar of his Foundry Hotel, Kalgoorlie, and his mind went back to the afternoon of 15 January 1931. He looked briefly at the huge lump of gold-painted plaster of paris on the wall and suddenly he seemed very far away.

"It was just after lunch," he said, "and my father was sitting under a tree. I was a lad of sixteen and I wasn't tired so I kept chipping away at the ground. About eighteen inches down I struck something pretty solid and I knelt down and pulled the earth away and had a look. Then I went over to my dad and said, 'I think we've got it, Dad.'

"We couldn't even guess how big it was so we got hold of a plank and a box. We put the plank over the box then we got hold of a 70-pound bag of sugar and put it on one end of the plank and we stuck the nugget on the other end. And the nugget was heavier than the bag of sugar—it weighed it right down."

It was the fabulous Golden Eagle nugget, the biggest ever found on the Western Australian goldfields—twenty-four and a half inches long, eleven and a half inches wide, and two and a half inches thick, and weighing just over 1,135 ounces.

They were poor people, like the thousands of others who flocked to the Larkinville goldfields, fifty miles south of Coolgardie, after Jimmy Larkin had found rich alluvial gold in 1929. The next day they took their nugget to Coolgardie and, on the trip across the desert, the germ of an idea formed. They would

HOTEL
FOUNDRY HOTEL
FOUNDRY
DRIVE-IN
BOTTLE-Dept.
FOUNDRY
HOTEL
DRIVE-IN
BOTTLE DEPT
DRIVE-IN BOT
HANNAN'
LIKE GOLD... SETS TH
DENVER CITY
HOTEL
SCAHILL'S
DENVER CITY HOTEL

Gold Mines Hotel, Bendigo, Victoria

Facing page: Young people outside the pub at Kuranda, Queensland

Above: Old beer sign, Somerton Hotel, New South Wales

Right: Bluestone Hotel, Inverell, Victoria

Facing page: TOP The Gainsborough Room, Largs Pier Hotel, South Australia. BOTTOM Northern Gateway Hotel, Port Augusta, South Australia

Above: A beer beside the pool, Walkabout Hotel, Newman, Western Australia

AD 1890
COMMERCIAL HOTEL
VICTORIA BITTER
O'CONNELL'S HOTEL
MEALS
BAR

PALACE
HOTEL
CROSSING

Facing page: TOP O'Connell's Commercial Hotel, Morang South, Victoria. BOTTOM The Palace Hotel, Broken Hill, New South Wales

Above: Lancefield Road Hotel, Clarkefield, Victoria

Somerton Hotel, New South Wales

become publicans, men of substance in those Depression days. Arthur Dunstan, whose parents had the Denver City Hotel in Coolgardie, remembers the nugget's arrival.

"They left it on the footpath outside the pub and went inside for tea. We kids were allowed to stay up late and I remember we danced around the nugget in our pyjamas." The Larcombes let everyone feast their eyes and later that night hid the nugget under the woodheap at the back of the pub. And the next day they took it to Kalgoorlie to a heroes' welcome.

Jim said: "Hannan Street was packed with people. What a day it was!" Within a few days they had sold the nugget for £5,431. They took a lease on the Grand Hotel in Hannan Street, Kalgoorlie and later bought the Terminus in Boulder and renamed it the Golden Eagle, a name it bears today. The Larcombes now have the Foundry in Boulder Road, where the plaster of paris replica on the wall is a daily reminder of the strike that put them in the hotel business.

Young Arthur Dunstan, who was ten when the Golden Eagle was found, went on to become a famous publican on the goldfields himself. He was born in the Denver City Hotel and it seemed there was no escaping the pub life. Now he has the old Railway Hotel in Perth and is Western Australian president of the Australian Hotels' Association. He is a great repository of goldfields tales.

"My family moved from Coolgardie to take over the Mount Lyell Hotel in Kalgoorlie and I was a twenty-year-old bank johnny when my father died in 1941. I took over the running of the pub, and my, those were tough times. The first trial wasn't long in coming. On Sunday I had to go out from behind the bar to talk to a bloke who was swearing heavily. I told him to quieten down, and he gave me a paternal slap on the back and ripped my shirt right off. So I grabbed his shirt and tore it off his back, and we were the best of mates after that." And so he became the friend, confidant, and creditor for some weird and wonderful people—Perc the camel driver, Plum Jam, Waistcoat Jack, Pickles. . . .

"Perc the camel driver had some sort of business picking up manure in a horse and dray, but he never failed to be in attendance at the pub at opening time. He was always the first in the door for the Sunday morning session. However there came one day when he didn't turn up. We waited fifteen minutes, then half an hour, and still no sign of him. Finally, after forty-five minutes, he dashed into the bar, and was out of breath. He didn't say a word but just tossed a note to me.

"The note was from his wife. It said: 'Dear Mr Dunstan, please excuse Percy for being late, but he had to chop some wood'!"

Indeed, the failure of Perc the camel driver to appear for the first round almost prompted a search party. There was the time that Arthur had asked the parson

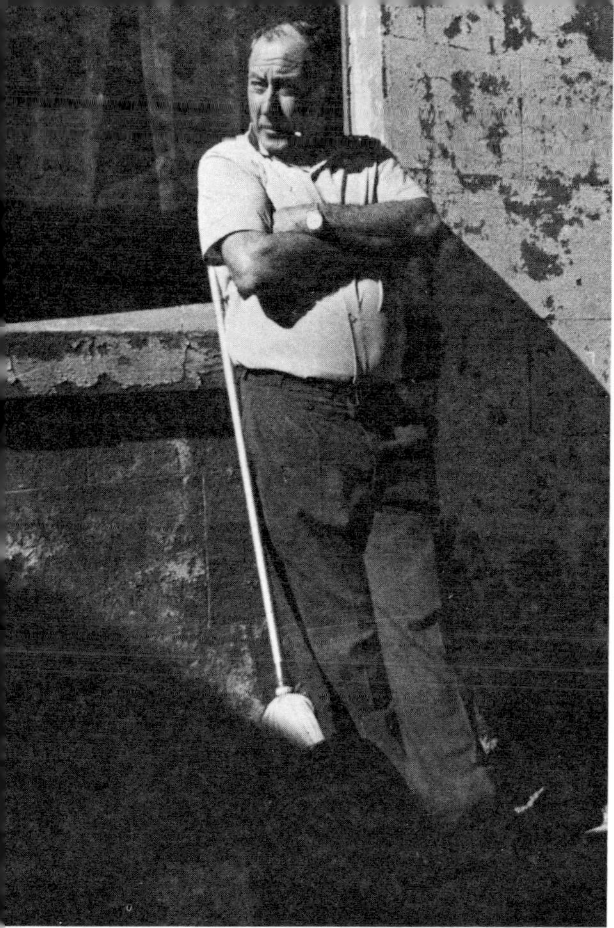

LEFT: Jim Larcombe. RIGHT: Arthur Dunstan

to come to the hotel early one Sunday morning to take his children to Sunday School. Percy was sunning himself in the gutter outside the public bar when the good clergyman, with his robes fluttering in the breeze, appeared and started to bang on the bar door.

Percy leapt to his feet, took up a position beside the astonished parson, and began thumping at the door furiously, too.

"Open up," he cried. "Open up, Arthur, the parson's feeling crook, too."

And there was the gentleman they knew as the Silent Knight who, once a week, rode his bicycle sixty-odd miles from Widgiemooltha to the brothels in Kalgoorlie. He will always be remembered for his remark in the bar of the Mount Lyell after he was asked whether it was a hard weekly trip. "It's not so hard gettin' there," he said. "But it's bloody hard gettin' home again." Yes, those ladies of pleasure in Kalgoorlie always gave a man his money's worth, even if it was to the detriment of his health.

Silent Knight was a lad in Widgiemooltha when a family named Doyle owned the pub. One day Mrs Doyle fell ill, and her husband had to decide whether she needed to go to the doctor in Kalgoorlie. No doctor would consider coming to Widgiemooltha. Anyway, he took a long look at his spouse and decided she was too far gone—she wouldn't survive the trip. So he measured her up for a coffin instead and sent someone to Kalgoorlie for it.

Of course, when the completed coffin arrived at the Widgiemooltha pub, Mrs Doyle was hale and hearty again. And Doyle, being a frugal man, used the coffin as a wash-trough for the beer glasses.

Later, less ghastly wash-troughs were installed, and the coffin was broken up to become shelves in the pantry.

Arthur said: "Isolation, like Widgiemooltha's, often caused problems. I remember once when the pub at Broad Arrow, north of Kalgoorlie, was cut off by floodwaters. They ran out of beer, and a bloke offered to try to get through to Kalgoorlie in his utility to replenish the supplies. He got to Kalgoorlie and threw two ten-gallon kegs of Hannans in the back and set off again for Broad Arrow. On the way he got hopelessly bogged and was at his wits' end until an ambulance, heading north, came to his aid. The ambulance blokes listened sympathetically to his problem and agreed to take the beer with them.

"Well, the scene changes to the Broad Arrow pub. The ambulance pulled up, and the driver leapt out, very briskly, and unloaded the two kegs of beer.

"There were two old-timers sitting on the verandah and one was heard to remark to the other: 'I always knew that Hannans beer was crook, but it's the first time I've ever seen it delivered in an ambulance.' "

Once upon a time Kalgoorlie was a long stopover on the Transcontinental Railway, and it became a matter of pride for some travellers to try to drink a beer in every pub in the main street while waiting for the train to depart. The locals had a profitable little trap for the unwary.

The tourist would walk into the Star and Garter, the bottom pub in Hannan Street. A local would eye him off and say: "I betcha can't start by drinking a teaspoonful of beer in this pub, then double up in every pub up the street."

"Easy," the tourist would inevitably say.

So he'd have a teaspoonful at the Star and Garter and, with a grinning crowd following, stroll uphill to Hannans, where he'd double up with two teaspoonfuls, or a dessertspoonful.

And so it went on: Kalgoorlie Hotel—one tablespoonful; York—one ounce; Oriental—two ounces; Commercial—four ounces; Victoria—one schooner (the local term for an eight-ounce glass); Palace—two schooners; Exchange—four schooners; Australia—eight schooners; Criterion—sixteen schooners; Grand—thirty-two schooners; Duke of Cornwall—sixty-four schooners; Federal—128 schooners. Or a grand total of 255 schooners plus sundry spoonfuls! It is not recorded whether anyone ever won his bet.

Arthur Dunstan said: "You don't hear much about the old pub crawl these days. Two of those pubs have gone, and the locals reckon they'd be risking their money if they bet someone they couldn't do it. We think there are a couple of blokes who could." After all, the total now would be a mere sixty-three schooners as well as the few spoonfuls.

Most of the old characters have gone now; even Plum Jam, a well-known Perth publican (known by no other name to the old goldfields crowd). Many of the great old pubs, particularly in Boulder, have gone. But in one case, Swan Breweries have made a marvellous effort to preserve the memory of a noted tavern—the Tower Hotel.

Like most of the hotels in the area, the Tower was built in 1899. Perched on the roof was an enclosed tower where the gentlemen of the town liked to play two-up and other games; they knew they would have an excellent view if the law appeared. In 1969 the brewery took over the pub and tore it down. In its place they built a fine new hotel and, as a concession to the past, named it the Tower and erected a false copper tower on the roof.

Above: The old Tower Hotel
Below: Tony Vickers and the new Tower Hotel

And in this sumptuous new hotel, they installed a man who would have held his own with ease in the Kalgoorlie of the wild old days.

Swedish-born Tony Vickers, in his thirties, is a former heavyweight boxing champion of Australia.

He said: "When I came here, it was like being the fastest gun in the West. They all wanted to try me out. I learned very quickly that Australian champions weren't recognised in Kalgoorlie—only the local champion. I had to fight some."

Asked if he had lost any fights, he shook his head and said: "I couldn't afford to."

And that is why the Tower Hotel, Kalgoorlie, is a remarkably peaceful place in which to drink.

The Broad Arrow Pub at dawn

Wilcannia

He squatted on the verandah of the pub at Wilcannia, and you'd have sworn he was 150 years old. But he was only sixty-odd and he had a Scots name, Alistair McDonald, or something like that. His voice was barely audible, and you didn't feel like pressing him. He was just one of a dozen Aboriginal men lurking aimlessly around the door to the back bar. It seemed that they were broke—"They'll have to wait 'til the social welfare cheques come in on the mail car next week before they can get pissed again," a white man explained.

Alistair McDonald wouldn't have gone into the pub (under the sign: GLASSES OUTSIDE MEANS NO BEER) if he'd won the lottery.

Two young Aboriginal men, who must have had jobs with the Department of Main Roads, made for the bar door jingling their coins and he whispered: "Don't go in there, boys, it'll do you no good." They were embarrassed but they shrugged their shoulders and ignored him, so he turned away.

"I was a bad drunk," he said, "but I haven't had one for five years. I went to the other pub here, and the bloke said, 'No, we don't have darkies in here,' and something happened inside me, and I thought 'Bugger it, why should I?' " Inside the bar where the whites drank and the Aborigines were only shadowy figures in the next room, I said: "Where's the toilet?"

The barman said: "You'd better go upstairs. The blacks use the one downstairs." So we finished our beers and drove to Tilpa.

The pub at Wilcannia, New South Wales

"They call this pub the school of tarts"

It is now time to expose Albert Herbert Brundell's most masterful ploy and, at the same time, explain why even the toughest men in the West balk at starting a brawl in his lounge bar.

Albert has a three-piece band in the lounge of his pub, the School of Arts, in Roma, Queensland, and, behind this band, there are many mirrors.

And when someone starts trouble, Albert leaps on to the stage, adopts a fighting posture, and roars: "Right-oh, we'll take the lot of you."

His potential protagonists stare at him in disbelief and depart hurriedly, because it seems they will have to fight a veritable platoon of Alberts. The mirrors play funny tricks, but there is more to Albert's pub than mirrors. He has massed barmaids. And it's not a trick done with mirrors. At any one time there'll be about eight fluttering back and forth in front of the bemused drinker. And when the beer-pouring slacks off for a time, they regularly burst into song, led by Miss Ruby on guitar.

"Eight lovely young ladies," Albert grinned.

And one of the eight giggled: "Some people call this pub The School of Tarts. Naughty, aren't they?"

ABOVE: School of Arts Hotel, Roma, Queensland

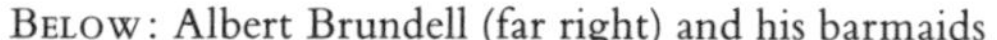

BELOW: Albert Brundell (far right) and his barmaids

The South

A year had elapsed since they smashed aside the last brick of James Byfield's beloved hotel to make way for a smart modern building, but his eyes were still damp. "Oh God," he said, "I cried for a month when I knew in my heart that the South Australian had to die." He sat stiffly in his sitting room on a pleasant Adelaide autumn morning, a man of great dignity and sensitivity, and it was clear that the old South Australian would never really die until James Byfield did.

Byfield, now the grand hotelier in spirit alone, spent much of 1972 selling out the famous O'Brien family's hotel interests—the South Australian had gone, to be followed by the Black Bull, Gresham, and Strathmore. Then he planned to fade into blessed obscurity on a twenty-three-acre farm near Northam, his hometown in Western Australia. A strange finale to the career of a man who once controlled one of the finest hotels in the land.

"I had reached a pinnacle, the ultimate as a hotelier," he said. "There was no future for me when the South had gone. I can't settle down to a different style of hotel, I simply can't erase the shadow of the South from my life. And no one will let me." Such is the hold that the South Australian had on its people. The O'Brien family, into which Byfield married, sold the old South Australian in May 1971, and they did not have a monopoly on the distress the sale caused.

For the South Australian Establishment and those who aspired to it, the hotel had become a living thing. When a wealthy grazier came to town, there was

no other place he would dream of staying. When the South went, there was confusion, and they were lost. What would they do? And the men who frequented the Terrace Bar, the politicians, the journalists, the influential, the well-known (and those who wished to be), where would they go? People were hurt, for the tradition of the South went back a long, long way.

The Terrace Bar was once the chamber of the Bank of South Australia, and when the hotel opened on the site in 1879 the bank vaults became its cellars. For many years the Flecker family owned it, and the redoubtable Mrs Flecker carved her name in the annals of the State's social history by crushing the actress Sarah Bernhardt in a conflict of wills. Bernhardt wanted her parrot to stay in the hotel with her; Flecker replied that if the parrot did not go, she would personally bounce Sarah from the pub. So the parrot went to the zoo.

But the hotel had its truly great moments when the O'Brien family owned it. The story began in the 1880s when one George Henry Read, a South Australian racehorse trainer, was attempting to secure stables in Melbourne. He had little success so he took over a hotel in Ascot Vale and billeted his horses there. Apparently having become interested in hotels, he returned to Adelaide and

Facing page: The South Australian Hotel

James Byfield

took a lease on the Black Bull in Hindley Street. He had a daughter, Louisa, who married John O'Brien. Subsequently Louisa and John took over the running of the Black Bull—and the name O'Brien was stamped for evermore on the State's hotel business.

In 1934 Louisa took the South Australian. James Byfield said: "She was the grand duchess of the hotel world; elegant, forthright, highly-respected, loved by her staff." She died on 16 September 1957, aged seventy-eight. Byfield, who had married her youngest daughter, Beth, was her logical successor; he was the cool hotelier, from his impassive face to his highly-polished shoes.

"It was an odd hotel," he said. "It started off as a sock and ended up as a sweater. It was a hotel which grew with the State. By virtue of the fact that it was continually added to and remodelled, its original air of grace remained. That is something you simply cannot get with rebuilding. At the end there were eighty-four rooms, and the most expensive suite cost seventy dollars a day. There were grand moments in our lives. We had the opportunity to speak to Queen Elizabeth, the Queen Mother, and the Duke of Edinburgh. Sir Robert Menzies and Dame Pattie were our guests. It's a great honour to have spoken to these people.

"The Beatles came and they were young gentlemen. At all times they were concerned that the clientele and conduct of the hotel were not interrupted because of their presence."

There were moments of crisis. "The most awful day was the earthquake of February 1954, the only earthquake of any consequence in South Australia for fifty years. There was a tremendous tremor and loss of power early in the morning. About 120 people were staying in the hotel at the time and they rushed about the corridors in their nightclothes, shrieking and crying. I recall that there were many New Zealanders staying with us, and they saved a lot of panic by walking quietly to the street and standing there. They were used to that sort of thing.

"I was dashing about and at one stage I passed the switchboard and noticed a light flickering, indicating that one of the guests was trying to contact the switchboard.

"I answered, and there was a lady calling from her room, very critical of the noise. She suggested that someone must be holding a raucous party.

"I said, 'Madam, there's just been an earthquake.'

"She replied, 'Don't be impudent, young man.' "

And the (ah hem) Bob Dyer Incident. "Mr Dyer, the television star, came into the dining room for high tea one Sunday wearing casual clothes—those days most decidedly frowned upon. He was wearing a sports jacket and trousers with a blue and white polka dot cravat tossed nonchalantly around his neck. I was sitting nearby and heard the headwaiter ask him if he would be good enough to go upstairs and put on a tie.

"Mr Dyer went upstairs and came down wearing a shoestring tie of the type favoured by gentlemen in the Wild West. He was admitted to the dining room, and we privately confessed among ourselves that he had scored off us. But in the long run, we scored too, because he never forgot the incident and always gave us a plug when a South Australian guest appeared on his show. He was never malicious—always a gentleman."

When the South Australian was sold, Byfield and his wife moved to the Black Bull, which George Read had bought freehold in 1891. Byfield was now playing the role of undertaker to the family's hotels but he did it with style. One of the features of the renovations that he carried out to the Black Bull was a bar for those wandering former patrons of the Terrace at the South Australian. It has a bull theme, with appropriate sketches on the wall—a bull cornering a cow in the paddock and the caption "Inescapa*bull,*" or a particularly lustful-looking bull titled "Insatia*bull.*"

James Chittleborough built the Black Bull in 1838 and at first named it the Buffalo, after the ship which brought him and his family from England the previous year. A board hanging above the pavement outside bears the legend:

The Bull is tame so fear him not,
So long as you can pay your shot,
When money's gone and credit's bad,
That's what makes the Bull go mad.

In 1947 the name of the Bull was changed to Berkeley ("for family reasons," Byfield smiled), but it returned to the original name in 1972. Although his last hotel home was the Bull, Byfield's great love will always be the South Australian.

"There were times when you thought your only friends were the cracks in the wall," he said.

Middleton

The pub at Middleton is a desperately lonely tin shelter, sharing the desolate landscape with two petrified tree trunks, some 700 miles north-west of Brisbane, or 250 miles north-east of Birdsville, whichever you prefer.

Now there's little to recommend the pub at Middleton apart from a rather novel little game they've invented. Behind the tiny bar, which also serves as a dispensing counter for sweets and groceries, stand two garbage bins. And above these garbage bins, there's a sign:

USED STUBBY DISPOSAL

Have a shot. If you miss you will be required to put 50 cents in the box for the Flying Doctor or the Crippled Children.

So when you've downed your stubby (it's unheard of to serve beer in glasses way out West!), you hurl it into one of the bins. Oh, it makes a very satisfactory smashing noise. But, as the night wears on, accuracy diminishes and, whoever's behind the bar must be frightfully agile.

But it all helps to break the monotony at Middleton.

Strippers

The George Hotel, St Kilda, any night, and Art Luden's ladies are getting their gear off. A sign outside says "This Is The Show" with the first letter of each word enlarged so much that anyone ten yards away reads it simply as TITS. The show on the first floor is a little more subtle. But not much more.

Comedian Ray Gibson bounces on to the stage: "Do you like my jacket?"

"Arr, get it orf!" The patrons are panting for skin.

"It's a present from my wife. I came home last night and found it hanging over a chair in our bedroom."

Ha, ha.

"My job's to tell you what goes on—and what comes off!"

Great mirth. Whistles.

"Now, give a big welcome to Mevina from New Zealand."

She had difficulty removing her gloves and everyone was becoming frightfully impatient. She had vast breasts.

Rosabella, from Scotland, had even vaster breasts.

"I'll marry ya tomorrow!" came a cry.

She showed us her most private place, and everyone let out a low whistle.

Gibson said: "That was one out of the box, wasn't it?"

Ha, ha.

A front row patron has returned to find someone sitting in his seat. He quickly reclaims it.

"This is the box seat!" he yells.

Ha, ha.

And finally, Jeanette Pleasure ("all the way from Paris").

She ate fire, showed us everything she owned, and Gibson had to remonstrate with a patron. "I'm paid to make a fool of myself," he said. "What's your excuse?"

Art Luden, a Sydney showman, brought his girls to Melbourne in 1971, to give the old town some much-needed culture. Now they're astonishing customers in the somewhat better-class Savoy Plaza as well as the George. Oh, there'd been strippers in Melbourne pubs before—Candy Barr, Autumn Leaves, and the rest at the Ritz in St Kilda. But they wore pasties and g-strings.

They didn't show us their . . . well. . . .

The tin shed

The last big herd went through in 1962, and Thelma Hawks watched their dust cloud fade into the east with tears in her eyes. The end had come for the pub on the Murrangi Track. Somehow she battled on for the next few years, though she knew all the time she would one day have to abandon the old place she loved.

In 1948 Thelma and her husband came to Top Springs on the southern fringe of Victoria River Downs, the world's biggest cattle station. They had an old truck and they hawked saddlery and stores to the drovers bringing the herds eastwards to the slaughterworks in Queensland.

In 1952 they built the pub, just a tin shed with a bar. And those were golden days. One year twenty-five mobs of cattle—with 1,350 head in each—passed through. But times changed, the beef road was built, and suddenly she discovered they were isolated, three miles from the passing traffic. Oh, the custom was still there. There were lonely men from the Victoria River Downs outstations at Moolloolloo and Pigeon and, often enough, from half a dozen road trains, each dragging four trailers of cattle. But it was not enough, and in the middle of 1972 she was preparing to leave the tin shed at Top Springs to the hungry desert and open a new roadhouse on the main highway a few miles away.

Another old pub was disappearing. Some of its character would go to the new place with Thelma. There were her faithful German Shepherd named Territory Mistake—"We thought his parents were spayed, but they weren't"—and the dusty trophy above the bar inscribed "The Hawks Perpetual Cup."

They bought it some years ago to present to the winners of a cricket match between Top Springs and Katherine, but the game did not eventuate. They tried to organise other games, but Top Springs was too far for teams to travel so the fine cup has never been contested.

Thelma was happy in the old pub, surely one of the most remote in Australia. "I'm alone now," she said, "but Territory Mistake always sleeps beside my bed, and I've never feared anything."

"See you at Weiley's..."

Billy ("Digger") Hill came quick marching home from the first World War with a message that set South Grafton a-talking.

Scrawled on the wall of the Trocadero Metro station in Paris, Billy saw the words:

"See you at Weiley's."

Weiley's had made it! Perhaps a lonely soldier's graffiti was not quite the advertisement that would put Weiley's in the same internationally-known class as the Ritz or the Waldorf. But in South Grafton, their chests swelled with pride. And then in the midst of the second World War, it happened again. This time it was a local lad, Clarrie Henderson, who brought the tidings. On the stern of a troopship in Cape Town, he saw painted: "When it's over, we'll have one at Weiley's."

Weiley's is the sort of pub a drinking man can fall in love with very quickly. Long, wide bars, the reflection of glasses on highly-polished counters, and the fan swinging idly overhead. The Weiley family opened the hotel and they have never relinquished control of it. The family's devotion to Grafton and its people is something to behold. They've produced two mayors and a State Member of Parliament, and the boys often bear the second Christian name: "Grafton."

The Weileys were a New South Wales pioneering family but they had concentrated their attention on other areas until 1889 when William James Weiley came to Grafton and opened the Globe Hotel. In 1909 he built the present Weiley's Hotel.

George Weiley, Grafton, New South Wales

The family's present patriarch, George, in his late seventies, is the most feared practical jokester for many miles around. And he relishes his captive victims, casual drinkers, and house guests. The locals still shudder over the incident during the visit of a waxworks show at the height of a flood. George agreed to store the waxworks figures in the safety of the hotel and was quick to notice they represented every murderer and unpleasant character ever to take breath (and, usually, have it choked off) in Australia.

So George, giggling all the while, took the monstrous figures and placed them in beds, behind doors, and in baths. His guests, mostly well inebriated, were the targets of his pranks. Their shrieks could be heard on the other side of the river.

At Weiley's there is a noted drinker who strictly obeys the orders of the

police not to drive his car home drunk. Instead, he weaves home on his bicycle.

It seems that one night, this gentleman (we'll call him Tom) was making an uneven progress home on his bike when it occurred to him that a police car was following. He was right, of course, but the police had no intention of arresting him. They merely wanted to reassure themselves that he would make it to his front door in one piece.

But Tom's guilt got the better of him. He suddenly leapt from his bike and bolted into the backyard of a house where he espied a hen house. He dived into the darkened hen house and stood ever so still, barely breathing.

A constable, in a very pleasant frame of mind, followed Tom into the backyard.

"Hey, Tom," he cried, "are you in that hen house?"

For a moment there was silence. Then a voice said: "No, constable, there's no one in here except us chooks."

Kulgera Hotel

Ah, there's no greater pleasure than the sight of a good outback dunny. Don Burgess who has the Kulgera Hotel, just above the border of the Northern Territory and South Australia, has created an architectural wonder.

"And the tourists complain," he sighed. More fools they are.

For the technically-minded: Corrugated iron exterior and what the proprietor describes as "a deep drop lav."

Furthermore, he adds: "If a tourist falls in, there are no worries. We just throw phenyl over him so he won't stink."

That dunny has a special role to play. It prevents the drinkers in the bar from the horrible sight of a rocky outcrop known to the Aborigines as the Weeping Eyes Rocks, a series of stepping-stone pools.

When Man gets into the forest, he does wondrous things.

The Markets Hotel Sydney

They wait outside at six-thirty in the morning, before the rest of the great city has risen from its slumbers. They rub their hands against the cold, and their leather aprons are already stained with the morning's exertions.

The doors open. Two beers, and they are back to humping their cases and fruit and vegetables and pushing their barrows. By nine they are back—"just for a couple more"—and so it goes on throughout the day.

In the Burlington Hotel, not far away, the sun is well short of the yard-arm but Aboriginal girls are already giggling over a game of snooker. A girl weeps on the pavement outside. Is she drunk already? Or just sad? No one takes any notice.

Beads for booze

The barmaid's name was Pauline Fisher. "The didgeridoos cost three dollars a foot," she said.

Below the didgeridoos on a shelf behind the bar were yards and yards of brightly-coloured beads.

"The Abos make them for flagons of booze," the barmaid said.

What length of beads for a flagon?

"Oh, about a mile," she grinned.

This is the Barrow Creek Hotel, Australia's most central pub, just forty-three miles north of Mount Stuart, the centre of the continent.

On the jagged stones behind the pub, four Aborigines were sitting. The two men were drinking from flagons of port. The women were making beads.

They are descendants of the Katish tribe, which attacked Barrow Creek telegraph station on 23 February 1874 and killed two white men.

They were once fierce warriors. Today they make beads and didgeridoos.

The Cavills

In the beginning the Cavills were swimmers. Then they became publicans.

Professor Fred Cavill once swam the English Channel and so impressed the Prince of Wales, later King Edward VII, that his powerful body was used as a model for a statue of the prince. They merely stuck Edward's head atop Fred's body.

Then in the early years of the century came the mighty Dick Cavill, the man who introduced the Australian crawl to competitive swimming. It was Dick Cavill who espied a rather barren stretch of coastline south of Brisbane and considered it an ideal place for surfing. And Surfers Paradise became Australia's holiday mecca. Today Cavill Avenue begins beside the Cavill's Surfers Paradise Hotel.

But it is Dick's nephew, Greg Cavill, who has perhaps the most popular pub in Brisbane, the Breakfast Creek Hotel. Breakfast Creek itself is somewhat foul and can-ridden these days, but the pub survives healthily. It is a weird, enchanting establishment with a fine staircase, vast beer gardens, and elderly bars unspoiled by vulgar renovators.

But it is also a pub with a split personality. In one bar some of the toughest citizens in Brisbane may be observed quaffing their ales, while a few yards away, through a door and beside the outdoor barbecue, solid people of impeccable reputation come to partake of the Breakfast Creek's famous lunch.

"We've had some of the biggest and best fights in Queensland here," Greg said, "but we do try to protect our better-class clientele from such events."

BOTTLE DEPT

Greg Cavill of the Breakfast Creek Hotel

Of course, many people recall the occasion when they very nearly failed. One day Pretty Micky from the wharves pursued a panic-stricken stevedore from the public bar into the exclusive outdoor restaurant and began sinking the slipper into him amid gasps and cries of "Oooh" and "Aaah." Greg removed Pretty Micky, took him outside, and threatened to demolish him. The wharfie was so astonished at the publican's temerity that he departed hastily.

"We had another blue here a couple of years ago. Two rival gangs met in the bar and fought it out. Oh, it lasted an hour, I suppose."

It was an exceptionally well-mannered fight, that one, according to eye-witnesses. Any drinker not involved in the gangs was left alone to sip his beer, immune from any nasty physical contact so long as he kept his body swaying with the crowd.

Greg stood beside a window where a previous publican had leapt to his death one afternoon (and by the sound of the place, who could blame him?).

"It's considerably quieter here now," he said. More's the pity.

Chloe of the west

Someone brought a painting of a girl in the nude to Grong Grong in south-west New South Wales, and Don Robertson, the schoolteacher, thought her a great beauty. So he bought her, and they put her on the wall.

In Grong Grong they'll tell you that story of how they came by the painting called "Chloe of the West." And they'll tell you about the funniest man for miles, the bloke who came to the pub one day and threw a snake on the bar. They all ran for their lives.

"It's nothing to be frightened of," the jokester spluttered through his tears of mirth. "Can't you weak bastards see that I've sewn its mouth up!"

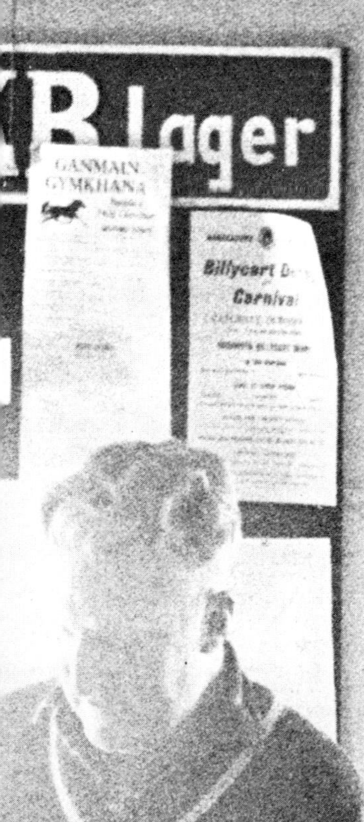
"Chloe"
OF THE WEST
Blager
GANMAIN
GYMKHANA
Billycart
Carnival

Jens

Johannes Matthies Jens and John "Black" Byng would seem to have little in common; they probably never met. But both left their mark on a street corner in Mount Gambier.

Byng was an American black with eighteen-inch biceps, a white wife, and seven children. In 1847 he erected the settlement's first commercial building on the corner of what is now Commercial Street and Watson Terrace.

It was a foul tavern, described by a contemporary observer as a "poverty-stricken public house lit with tallow candles." Later he sold out to Alexander Mitchell who built the Mount Gambier Hotel on the site. In turn, Mitchell sold the site to a gentleman named Ginger Beer Jack, who ran a boarding house there until . . . enter the refined Johannes Matthies Jens, a German immigrant.

Jens wanted to tear down the boarding house and build a fine hotel, but the police, seven other publicans, temperance groups, and members of the public opposed his plan. He finally won, and when Jens Hotel opened in 1884 it was lit by gas, and the balcony was festooned with Chinese lanterns.

Today Jens is still a fine hotel, with a sombre foyer and wide stairs leading to large rooms. It has a fine reputation, particularly among the landed gentry. J. M. Jens would probably be horrified to have his establishment associated with "Black" Byng.

But then Byng probably would not have considered Jens' pub much fun.

JENS

Lightning Ridge

Harold Hodges, septuagenarian opal buyer, recalled the bad old days: "We did all our dealin' in the pub, and the miners'd come in and wait till us buyers were half drunk. Then they'd come up and show us their stones hopin' they'd get a better deal if we were full. But we educated 'em out of that. We got 'em to come to our huts with the stones. It was no good tryin' to buy stuff in the pub. You couldn't have a good look at a stone without some bludger lookin' over your shoulder. Everyone knew your business. But these days we've even educated the miners to acceptin' cheques."

The Diggers Rest Hotel in Lightning Ridge is the only oasis in the black opal country; it is a classic, low, wooden Australian bush pub. The Sceats family came to Lightning Ridge in the early 1960s to search for opal and finished up running the pub. It's a deceptive place; out the back and behind the little front bar crowded with miners in safety helmets, there's a splendid lounge complete with stage.

Harold Hodges came to Lightning Ridge way back when only twenty-five or so men were burrowing through the sandhills. "Then, as now, the pub meant the world to us. It was our only amenity. Crikey, it was rough, though. I was standing at the bar one day when a bloody emu walked in the door and took a sip out of my beer."

When he's not breasting the bar, Harold can be found at his Tram Motel, a few hundred yards down the track. A quaint name, you might say, for a motel several thousand dustbowls from the nearest tram tracks. But not so. The story of the Tram Motel began in the pub one afternoon later in 1960.

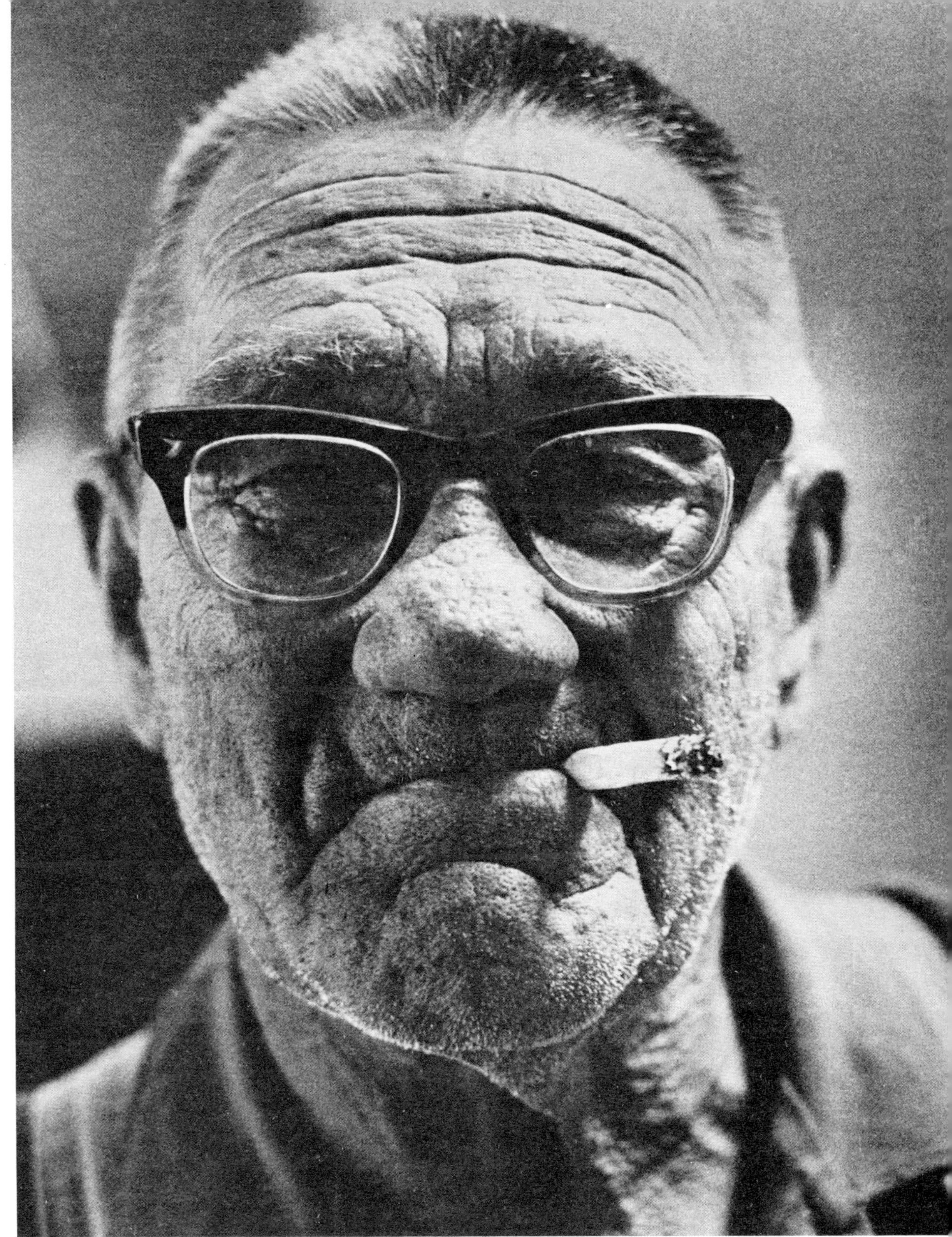

Harold Hodges, Lightning Ridge

"We were havin' a few beers," Harold said, "and I bet some bloke that the kids in Lightning Ridge would all have a tram ride by the first of February 1961. Jeez, they all laughed! But they all looked pretty stupid when I brought two trams from Sydney on semi-trailers, and all the kids climbed into the trams, and the semis drove around town. I won thirty-eight quid. Anyhow, it seemed a bloody good idea so I got another five trams from Sydney and Melbourne and turned 'em into motel units. I would have got more, but the bloody shire council stopped me. Yep, all the best things in town start in that pub. I saw a bloke sell a stone there for 3,000 quid and only eight days later he was trying to bludge a free drink. Dead broke, he was."

Although there are about 800 miners working in and around Lightning Ridge, the Diggers Rest Hotel is not exclusively a miners' pub. It's the nearest watering hole for stockmen on the big stations nearby.

"They're thirsty blokes," David Sceats said. "One bloke came here one day driving a truck full of sheep. He stopped at the pub, went in, had a beer, then another. It came lunchtime, then mid-afternoon, and he was still knocking 'em down. Someone said to him, 'Hey mate, it's bloody hot out there. Don't you reckon you oughta give them sheep a drink?'

"The bloke was very full. He thought for a minute and said, 'You're dead right, mate,' and he threw a fiver on the bar and said, 'Give me thirty whiskies.'

"So he took 'em out to the sheep on a tray and tried to make them drink. But they wouldn't. So he chucked the whisky over them and said, 'That oughta cool the bastards off.' "

The Albion, Forbes

Below the public bar of the Albion lies a vast, untidy cellar. The cellar floor is damp and treacherous, and in the dim recesses are unkempt fireplaces. Something happened here.

And below this cellar, in the mud, slush, and clay around the pub's foundations, is something more. A reef of gold, or so they say.

On the roof of the hotel is a tower, the highest point in the town, and it was from here that anxious eyes scanned the distant bush for the Cobb & Co coaches. They had good reason to be anxious, for this was Ben Hall country. On 5 May 1865 a blacktracker, Billy Dargin, shot the bushranger dead, and they buried him in Forbes cemetery; the grave is not hard to find because unknown persons have tended it faithfully. The romanticism of Ben Hall haunts Forbes today.

The Albion is also very much a part of Forbes' romantic past. It was built in 1861 and rebuilt in 1867, but an old local knows the story better: "There was rich alluvial gold here, and when they were rebuilding the pub, the workmen struck a reef under one corner. They wanted to abandon the pub and start a mine, but the publican would have nothing of that. He's supposed to have paid 'em off to be quiet about it."

The Albion Hotel, Forbes, New South Wales

Mrs Mary Healy, who had the hotel recently, said: "I believe there's gold down there, and my brother, F. P. Walsh, a civil engineer, wanted to pump the cellars out so we could get at it. But it came to nothing! The gold will probably stay there for ever."

It was easy to understand why that publican long ago preferred to have his hotel finished rather than enter the chancy business of gold mining. The real money was in beer. The old local said: "Y'know that cellar underneath? Well, fifty-odd years ago, that was a special bar for squatters. They were an arrogant breed, thinking themselves men above the rest—and big men they were. Some of them were using a hundred shearers those days. Well, they gathered down in that cellar—and it was an opulent place then—and drank all night and carried on like madmen, smashing things. In the morning, they thought nothing of paying for the damage. They had plenty of money. They went there to be alone; they wouldn't drink with the ordinary townspeople."

The fight

The whites, congregated along the verandah, were joking, sipping their beers, and watching the two Aboriginal boys slug it out. Hopelessly drunk, they were just slapping each other and barely causing pain. Everyone smiled and thought it a bit of a laugh.

Jimmy-Jimmy was tiring of the fight and wanted to wander away, but an old Aboriginal man with a walking stick thrust him back into the circle. Soon the whites, too, became bored and drifted back to their stools at the bar, for it was merely another night in Fitzroy Crossing.

A cool evening breeze drifted unhindered through the bar. The pub at Fitzroy Crossing is unique in that it has no doors or even walls. Simply a roof with pillars

and a U-shaped bar. At closing time they take away the cash tray and cigarettes and cover the pool table. And when the people have gone and the lights are dim, shadowy figures often creep in to sleep on the floor.

Jimmy-Jimmy lurched into the bar; he was bare-chested, part-Aboriginal, part Thursday Islander. "He's stirred," someone said, but they turned away and ignored him.

An Aboriginal, perhaps aged forty, was sitting on a stool. He wore a stockman's hat and he was very drunk.

"You black bastard!"

The whites turned slowly and saw Jimmy-Jimmy standing by the man in the stockman's hat. Jimmy-Jimmy's eyes were aflame, and this time the whites did not ignore him.

"You black bastard!" Jimmy-Jimmy's voice was shrill.

He lashed out, and the stockman toppled from his stool as if in slow motion, bounced against the bar, and slithered to the floor.

Twice Jimmy-Jimmy kicked him in the ribs with his bare feet.

Twice he raised his right heel and cracked the stockman's head on the concrete. Men came and dragged the angry boy away.

In a corner, a little white boy, the cook's son, trembled, and his eyes filled with tears.

Beside the prostrate body, a white man with red hair was still drinking his beer. He looked straight ahead, and his eyes did not waver for an instant. Another white man said: "Let the bloody blacks sort it out. The good blacks will sort it out."

Jimmy-Jimmy was weeping now. He threw himself on his knees before the whites and opened his arms like a supplicant.

"I love you white people," he sobbed. "Oh, man, I love you. You gave me my education."

Again he was gone into the night—and again he returned. The tears had passed, and the fury distorted his face again. He shrieked abuse at the Aborigines, and a tall Thursday Islander passed his pool cue to his white girlfriend and began pulling off his blue shirt and exposing a fine chest. In the confusion Jimmy-Jimmy slumped to the floor by courtesy of a sharp jab from another Islander. He lay there, whimpering, until the stockman he had attacked earlier drew himself from the floor and stumbled back on his bar stool again.

Jimmy-Jimmy lunged at him again, but strong arms held him back. "It was ten against one, you bastard," Jimmy-Jimmy cried. "You come to the reserve tonight, man, and we'll settle this with a spear fight!"

A policeman came and took him away. His parting cry drifted into the bar: "I think they're taking me to jail!"

A white man said, taciturnly: "You can say that again, mate."

The publican, Trevor Bidewell, had come running from the store adjacent to the hotel. "It's just an average night," he sighed.

Despite the occasional tragic scenes enacted in the bar, it's a fine pub at Fitzroy Crossing. Every afternoon they pour 400 gallons of water, pumped from the river, on to the lawn to maintain the greenness cherished by outback people.

The morning after the fight, the first barmaid on duty reported that the bar cloths had been stolen, but with no doors or walls to protect them, it was hardly surprising. The first drinkers were assembling shortly after nine.

Down the road Jimmy-Jimmy was pacing the cage-like cell behind the police station; he was waiting for a Justice of the Peace to arrive from a cattle station.

It's not pleasant to have to tell a story like Jimmy-Jimmy's. But it happened in a pub in Australia.

The pub with no beer

The Palace Hotel at Southern Cross, one of the oldest on the trail of the Western Australian goldfields, surrendered its licence in the mid-1960s. Today it still stands proudly as a fifty-one-room fortress of red brick. The beer signs are still there, and the bar is still there.

But the pub's got no beer. It's a boarding house now, in fact.

So it seems appropriate that Slim Dusty, that ol' country boy, should be found sitting mournfully on his guitar outside the old place.

"Used to be one of my favourites," he yodelled, "it's getting so that all the old places are fading away. Why, me and my wife Joy have taken to staying in motels these days when we're on tour."

Motels! What sacrilege!

Yes, tragic, because Slim and his guitar made the outback pub famous all over the world through the song, "The Pub With No Beer."

Slim Dusty outside the pub with no beer

"Clancy of the Overflow"

Glenn Clancy's no more than a slip of a fella, but they say he's the fightingest man west of the Barcoo. Oh, he's no fool, that Clancy (I mean, there can't be too many outback publicans named Clancy who'd have the imagination to call their pub Clancy's Overflow Hotel as a tribute to the great bush poet Banjo Paterson and his drover character, Clancy).

Now, Banjo Paterson himself would be proud of Clancy lording it over his customers in his pub at Isisford, on the banks of the Barcoo River, which is always dry except when it overflows. There are few nights when you won't find Clancy trading blows with some obstreperous customer and having perspiration running down his Irish face. It appears that Clancy the publican, like Clancy the drover, doesn't use his first name. He's known universally by his surname.

"Come out from behind that bar and fight, Clancy! I'll smash ya to ribbons, you little bastard!"

So Clancy, not being one to bother the constables, invariably obliges.

"Gawd, we had a nice little dust-up in here a while ago," he said. "The fella who makes the sausages over the road at the butcher's came in here, put a bloody great parcel of snags on the bar, and started calling me for everything under the sun. So I went out from behind the bar and had a punch-up with him and finally chucked him out the back door and locked it. But I'd forgotten that the front door had been knocked off its hinges in another blue earlier in the night, and the big bastard came charging through and went at me again. And you know who won the second fight?—the bloody drover's dog, that's who.

"It was over, more or less, and we were all lying on the floor, everyone in the bar. And I looked up, and there was a train of sausages disappearing around the corner and, when we looked, the dog was sitting there, bolting 'em down, one at a time. Jeez, the bloke from the butcher's did his block. The rest of us couldn't stop laughing!"

They like a little joke between bouts out there on the Barcoo.

ABOVE: The road to Isisford, Queensland

On the Barrier Reef

Well, they'd planned to demolish the old pub anyway. But not quite with the savagery of the wild, wild woman named Althea who came out of the sea. At one moment, the old wooden Hotel Magnetic on Picnic Point, Magnetic Island, was standing. The next moment, it was a heap of kindling, one of the first victims of the fury of Cyclone Althea on 24 December 1971.

We were there not long before Althea came. It was a superbly peaceful day to be sitting in the shade of the old pub (not thinking for a moment that in a very few weeks it would be blown down); a big red flower, however, obscured our view of the sea. Time matters nought on the Barrier Reef islands, and Magnetic Island, in particular, has become a refuge for the old folk ("the only place where the dead are allowed to walk around," goes the local joke of doubtful taste).

But Queensland pubs and cyclones have always had an unhappy relationship. There's the Half Sovereign in Cooktown—that's right, it was once called the Sovereign until a cyclone swept away half the public bar. And the West Coast at Cooktown. A pub named the West Coast situated on the east coast?

Well, the true story is that the West Coast was once at Broome, in Western Australia. But one night a cyclone blew it all the way to Cooktown, and it opened for business there the following morning. And no one's got around to changing the name. Oh, by the way, one can't talk about the West Coast without

giving some mention to the famous duo they had performing in the lounge some time ago, a dog and a crocodile. The dog played the piano, and the crocodile sang.

Anyway, it so happened one night that an important representative from the theatrical firm, J. C. Williamson's, was in Cooktown, and he saw this act performed.

"Sensational!" he cried, throwing his hands in the air. "I must sign them up."

"Ya can't," said the publican.

"And why not, pray tell?"

"Ya just can't."

"My dear man, I'm distraught, I must have that act. Please, please, tell me why I can't."

"Orright, I'll tell ya. It's a phony act."

"What!" The theatrical man could hardly believe it. He stared at the dynamic duo. The dog's fingers flickered across the keys; the crocodile sang like Nellie Melba.

"What do you mean—it's a phony act?"

"Yeah, that's right. The croc can't sing—the dog's a ventriloquist!"

The Commercial

Nothing held greater promise, yet left more scars, than gold.

In 1859 the Commercial in Braidwood was spawned by the feverish search for the yellow escape.

The last gold dredge left Braidwood thirty years ago.

In the bar at the Commercial, they've a picture of the grand old days when Cadillacs were parked outside.

The few that come to the pub now do not even bother to look at the picture any more.

The little pub

Max David, a Berliner with a remarkable capacity for Scotch whisky, fought for Rommel and then the French Foreign Legion, but he always nursed a better idea.

"I wanted a little pub," he said.

Well, he got his little pub, but something went wrong: it turned into a big pub (while always remaining a little pub, y'see).

Six years ago Max and Latvian-born Vic Zirnis took over the Old Queen's Arms at the corner of Wright and Compton streets, Adelaide. It first opened in March 1839—the sixth official licence to be issued in South Australia. The Old Queen's Arms, from the outside, is just a little corner pub, two storeys, with exquisite lacework on the balcony.

Inside, it's a monster.

What happened was that Max, who runs the pub, decided he would make a specialty of meals, particularly lunches. Word passed around, and soon they were all trooping down—"Don Dunstan, the Premier, comes here, so does Steele Hall, and often Whitlam when he's in town," Max said. Suddenly Max found he was doing 1,000 meals a day and needed three kitchens so he expanded sideways, buying the two cottages next door. From the exterior they still look like cottages, but inside they are part of his rambling dining area.

Old Queen's Arms Hotel, Adelaide

Max won the Iron Cross serving with the Afrika Corps' 19th Light Division as a despatch rider. The British caught him and freed him on condition that he fought with the French Foreign Legion. He came to Australia in 1951 and soon had his own coffee shop.

He claims a special distinction for his English-born wife, Olive: "She is the only Englishwoman to have been presented with the Iron Cross," he said. "In 1971 she went to Berlin for a holiday and collected my Iron Cross on my behalf. How do you think Churchill would have liked that, eh?"

Footnote: The Old Queen's Arms is noted for its tasty barmaids, too.

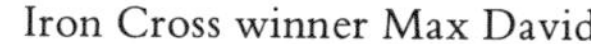

Iron Cross winner Max David

Gin Gin

Two brothers, Bert and Laurie, drink at the pub at Gin Gin, and it is their habit to transport themselves to the hotel in a sulky drawn by a mare.

But one night some humorists ran off with the mare, a fact discovered by the brothers when they came weaving into the night after closing time.

Bert said: "Well, Laurie, looks like you'll have to pull the cart 'ome."

So Laurie, somewhat sulkily, got between the shafts and began the drunken tow home. Bert, of course, rode in the sulky but had enough good taste not to use the whip on his dear brother.

Anyhow, it happened that a constable in a car saw their drunken progress and came alongside them.

"Oi," he called to the panting Laurie, "what do you mean by weaving all over the road?"

"Don't blame me, constable," said Laurie, "I'm only the bloody horse!"

Marlborough Hotel, central Queensland

The little lady schoolteacher was positively outraged by the swearing at the pub (though she did admit that "bull" was allowable, this being the heart of the Brahmin country). So she put a large bottle on the bar:

SWEAR BOTTLE.

IN AID OF TRIP TO DARWIN.

It would be nice to report that she raised sufficient money for the fare in three or four bawdy nights. But, alas, barely a coin was dropped into the bottle.

"Y'see," said the barmaid, "if you don't contribute, we hit you over the head with the bottle." And it turned out the local blokes preferred a sore head to parting with their cash.

PUBL

Shearers

In the good old days when the shearing shed at Tinnenburra was the biggest in the world, Annie Lack's arms grew tired just opening beer bottles. But the shed is disused, silent now. The shearers have gone—but Annie, in her seventies, remains behind the bar of Tattersall's Hotel at Barringun, a mile south of the Queensland border.

"Sometimes," she sighed, "I mightn't sell a beer all day."

She occupies herself by keeping alive the outback oasis around the pub; the grass is green and soft underfoot, and flowers always bloom. Her husband, James, sits at the switchboard in the tiny post office they run next door. He has a full-size billiard table in a room behind the bar. But who's there to play?

Adjoining the corner bar, there's the Tap Room. Except there are no taps. "Oh, that's easily explained," Annie said. "The shearers used to sit around a table in that room, and when they wanted another jug of beer, they'd tap the wall."

The black soil

When the rain comes down and the black soil of north-central Queensland turns to glue, it is considered polite to remove one's shoes before entering the pub. On some pub verandahs, like this one at Maxwelton, the uninformed visitor could be excused for believing he was about to enter a mosque.

Prairie

"What are ya lookin' so upset about, mate?"

"Oh, we've been stuck in the mud out west for about fifteen hours."

"Could've been worse."

"How?"

"You could've been stuck there the rest of ya life."

"Suppose you're right."

If you can cope with this level of outrageous rural wit, then a visit to the Prairie pub in Queensland is exceedingly well worthwhile. For there is a client of this hotel, one Alan Scanlon, who actually saw the incident involving the Wild Irishman in Birdsville all those years ago.

"Yep, I was there," he said. "They didn't have a lockup in Birdsville those days, and the Wild Irishman had been playin' up. So the cops arrested him and chained him to a bloody great log outside the pub. Anyway, the sun beat down and after a couple of hours, the pub door burst open. And there was the Irishman with the log still chained to him, 'cept he was carrying it on his shoulder.

" 'It's bloody hot out there,' he said, 'how about givin' me a little drink?' "

PRAIRIE HOTEL

Personalities at the Prairie Hotel, Queensland

Dajarra

The public bar of the Dajarra Hotel has several paintings of nudes with breasts like helium balloons. They're all Aboriginal girls, lounging in sensuous repose around campfires. But who are they?

"Aw, just a few local girls," said a patron. Wink, wink, wink.

The truth is that they are the products of the fertile mind of a Mount Isa miner named Mickey Rooney (truly) who regularly makes the ninety-nine-mile trip south to Dajarra to paint in the bar. Using ordinary house paint, he sets up his canvas on two tea chests in a corner of the bar and paints away steadily all week-end, consuming large amounts of beer between each stroke of the brush.

The local people think he is marvellous.

"See the picture of that sheila there?" one whispered. "Well, it took him a whole quart of paint just to do her left tit."

ABOVE: Bath-tub cooler, temporary bar, Dajarra races, Queensland

LEFT:
One of the
nude paintings,
Dajarra Hotel

The Leap

The little pub stands at the foot of a 1,180-foot rock face, just north of Mackay, Queensland. The mountain's correct name is Mount Mandarana, but the local people call it The Gin's Leap. And that is how the pub came to be named The Leap.

Back in 1866–67, the local tribes were making life difficult for the early settlers by spearing cattle and stealing farm implements. After a destructive raid in July 1867, the police decided, with the aid of the farmers, to mount an offensive against the Aborigines. As usual, the Aborigines retreated to their fortress on the summit of Mount Mandarana, hitherto inaccessible to the police. But the troopers were determined this time and eventually succeeded in gaining the top.

The Aborigines fled, with the exception of a woman, Kowaha, of the Lindeman Island tribe. She was cornered with her baby in her arms and rather than surrender she hurled herself and her baby over the cliff. Kowaha died on the rocks below but, miraculously, the baby became ensnared in bushes during the fall and survived. A farmer rode through a hail of spears to rescue the child, and his family later adopted her. She became known as Judith Johannesburg and lived in the district until her death in 1923.

LEAP
HOTEL

Marble Bar

In the hottest town of the driest continent, the wandering drinker may find a great disappointment. The bar at Marble Bar isn't marble at all. So much for one great Australian myth.

How many times have tourists bounded into the bar of the Ironclad Hotel, their eyes aglow with joyous anticipation, to find . . . *that the bar is topped with aluminium.*

The Ironclad Hotel, so named because it sits upon a ridge of iron ore, is proudly owned by a family named Johnston. Once the Johnston boys were miners in the hills around Marble Bar and were trying to eke a living from the unyielding earth. Mrs Phil Johnston, wife of the licensee, Bob Johnston, said: "The boys vowed that if they ever struck it rich, they'd buy the pub. After all, that was where they spent all their money."

And they struck it rich. Now, as well as the pub, they have a mine, garage, and store.

Strangers anxious to rough it at the Ironclad Hotel these days will find it difficult. The bar is air-conditioned, there's a smart dining room, and Mrs Johnston labours to keep alive a garden beside the motel units. Oh, for the bad old

days! She said: "It wasn't always so civilised. I remember once when it was 117 degrees in the bar. We tried makeshift air-conditioning. We put a wire screen packed with spinifex in front of a fan and ran water over the spinifex. It worked for a little while, until the spinifex collapsed."

They're uncertain of the pub's history—so much has been added to, and taken away from, the original building. But they do know that the dining-room section of the building is at least eighty-seven years old. Whoever built the place committed an architectural blunder. The building is largely made of galvanised iron and, instead of placing it with the corrugations running downwards, they run across. It's a devil of a task removing the dust.

And the marble bar itself? That's a reef of rock spilling across a creek bed about two miles from the town. It looks something like marble but is actually jasper, and shines with a multitude of colours when it is wet. The pools among the sand nearby bear the proud title: Marble Bar Swimming Pool.

The unlikely pub

The night we came to Newman, we'd hit a giant kangaroo about thirty miles north. We crept those last miles into the town, wondering what awful internal injuries the car might have suffered. Our nerves were taut; it was bad enough having to watch the old 'roo die—we had also to watch for his brethren.

What sort of a place was this mining town of Newman? It mattered little; a meal, any sort of meal, and a bed would do. What more could a man expect on these harsh, ironclad mining ridges of the north-west. But there was something about Newman.

An old prospector out near Marble Bar had talked with some awe of the pub at Newman: "Gawd, mate," he said, "it's twenty-five dollars a night a single, and that doesn't count breakfast!"

Oh, yeah, you're having us on!

So we came to Newman—and didn't dare go into the bar until we'd showered and shaved. Such was the style of the pub at Newman—a most unlikely pub in a most unlikely place. A giant, rambling hacienda; suites whispering gentle piped music and looking on to genuine green grass; and sophisticated little bars tucked into nooks of white brick.

The pub at Newman (centre of picture)

The old prospector was mistaken. The suites were a mere fifteen dollars a night, but even that was enough to prompt a low whistle of amazement in these parts. But it was worth it! From the dining room, guests could interrupt their mastications to gaze upon others lazing around the pool to a backdrop of richly-coloured flowers, drooping from the white brick wall. A closer glance would reveal that the giant blonde, seated on the pool's edge and reading a novel, was permitting a pair of bountiful breasts to wink pinkly through a see-through bikini top. Indeed, there was nothing retarded about the local tastes in fashion. The barmaids were a treat—nearly all of them imports from Perth.

The Walkabout Hotel, Newman, is part of a chain bringing city luxury to the booming north-west—at Laverton, Gove, and Port Hedland. Much like the splendid Parmelia in Perth, they are progeny of Western Australia's mineral discoveries. The Newman pub was born with the town; it was opened on 20 December 1968, just a month before the Mount Newman mining company railed its first iron ore to the waiting ships at Port Hedland. Today the hotel—a white colossus built from bricks made of local sand—squats among the smart, brick, company houses. That mining is thirsty work is proved by the bottle sales alone on Christmas Eve, 1971. The town (population 2,700) spent $5,375 in the bottle shop!

The miners went through 140 kegs, one hot week, standing five deep at the bar. And it was about this time that the pub set an Australian record for beer sales. The pride on the surviving drinkers' faces was a sight to behold! In case they ever plan to improve on their record, the hotel has thirty-nine staff, including ten barmaids, standing by to help.

Christie

It was easy to see he was a hot-shot; he had his own cue which he'd imported from the Big Smoke and he handled it with loving ease—the sort of relationship you'd expect to see between a great violinist and his Stradivarius. He kept the cue behind the bar in a smart white bag and when the barmaid passed it to him, she handled it almost with reverence. For this was Christie, and he was a big man in these parts. Just Christie, no other name—he didn't need one.

Sunset at the Meekatharra Hotel, Western Australia

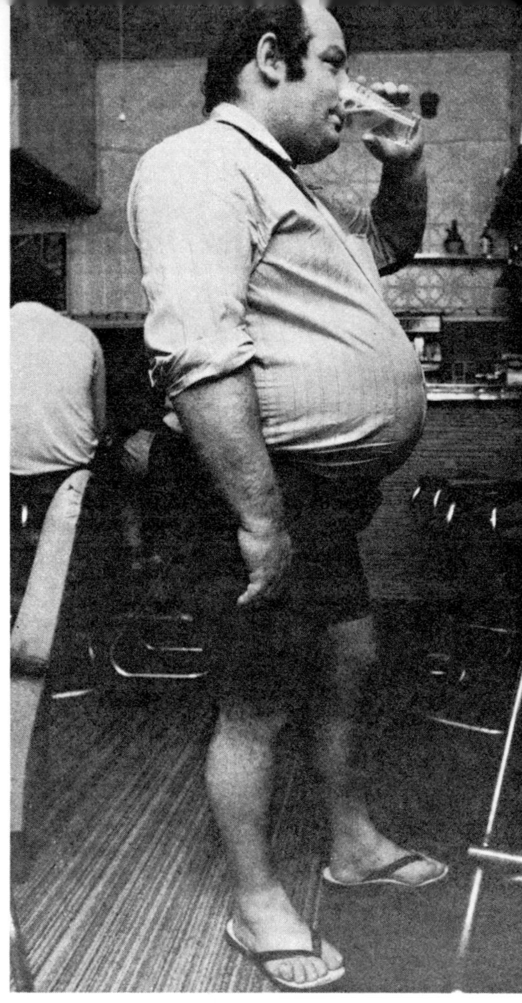

LEFT: John, the cook, Meekatharra Hotel
Facing page: Christie

He was twenty-five, dressed all in black, recently a rouseabout but now learning shearing; he was dark-skinned, gentle, and smiling. He came to the Meekatharra Hotel at five-fifteen sharp and put his twenty cents down to challenge for the table. He held it all night, except for the two times he potted the black off the break (of all things!).

You challenged him, although you knew it was hopeless. He toyed with you; you just missed a pocket, and he cried, "Oh, jolly good shot" or "Bad show," and you thought may be he was sending you up but you couldn't take offence. He pocketed your twenty cents and called for the next victim and, by the end of the night, you guessed he must have collected around four or five dollars. It didn't take Christie long to finish a game. Throughout the entire evening he drank only two glasses of beer. That was one of his rules.

He had two others: "I only play for money and I only ever play on this table. Oh, yes, I know about those two hot-shots up at Newman. They came here, and I cleaned one up for fifty bucks and the other for a hundred. Ready for another game?"

White Horse Hotel

Norm Kelly knew there was tin in that hill; he knew it deep in his heart. But he was out prospecting with his uncle, who was the boss, and he said, "No." So they went fossicking somewhere else.

Then two men came and found tin by the ton in Norm's hill. They became wealthy men. But Norm never quite made it, and now he sits in the White Horse in Charters Towers and pours out his soul to anyone who'll listen.

"I'd be a millionaire today," he said, "but maybe there's still a chance. I reckon I still know where there's a reef of gold."

"Hebel's leading hotel"

Once there were three things in Hebel, Queensland (not counting the dust). There was the Commercial Hotel (HEBEL'S LEADING HOTEL, says the sign outside), there was the store, and there was a pile of empty bottles which rivalled the pyramids of Egypt in size. Why, it was said that on a sunny day you could see them a-glittering from the Pacific coast, 350 miles east.

But one day the council made them bury the bottles.

And now there are only two things in Hebel (not counting the dust).

His first for the day, Hebel

Kingoonya Hotel

"Where's the next pub?" the traveller asks.

"Well, keep goin' straight ahead on this road and you'll strike one in two hundred and eight miles," the garage man says.

But it's worse than that! Two hundred and eight and a *half* miles, as the traveller discovers, for he's been gazing upon his speedometer, and his tongue has been slack, for mile after desolate mile.

As he presses desperately forward, leaving a great cloud of bulldust behind his flying wheels, he begins to suffer from mental mirages. There'll be swaying palms and a beer garden sheltered by an ancient vine. And there'll be topless barmaids to caress his fevered brow. And his beer will be so cold his teeth will ache. Ah!

But he finds Kingoonya, and there's no shade, no beer garden, and the barmen are wearing shirts.

Who cares? Beer tastes the same anywhere.

The barman says: "You've come up from Port Augusta?"

The traveller nods, for if he speaks he'll stop the flow of the medicinal amber fluid.

"Long way between drinks," the barman observes.

Too bloody right, the traveller thinks.